ISBN 978-1-330-51602-7
PIBN 10072456

1 MONTH OF
FREE
READING

at

www.ForgottenBooks.com

By purchasing this book you are
eligible for one month membership to
ForgottenBooks.com, giving you
unlimited access to our entire
collection of over 700,000 titles via
our web site and mobile apps.

To claim your free month visit:

www.forgottenbooks.com/free72456

English
Français
Deutsche
Italiano
Español
Português

www.forgottenbooks.com

Mythology Photography **Fiction**
Fishing Christianity **Art** Cooking
Essays Buddhism Freemasonry
Medicine **Biology** Music **Ancient
Egypt** Evolution Carpentry Physics
Dance Geology **Mathematics** Fitness
Shakespeare **Folklore** Yoga Marketing
Confidence Immortality Biographies
Poetry **Psychology** Witchcraft
Electronics Chemistry History **Law**
Accounting **Philosophy** Anthropology
Alchemy Drama Quantum Mechanics
Atheism Sexual Health **Ancient History**
Entrepreneurship Languages Sport
Paleontology Needlework Islam
Metaphysics Investment Archaeology
Parenting Statistics Criminology
Motivational

THE

PERFECT LIFE.

IN

TWELVE DISCOURSES.

BY

WILLIAM ELLERY CHANNING, D.D.

EDITED

FROM HIS MANUSCRIPTS,

BY

HIS NEPHEW,

WILLIAM HENRY CHANNING.

BOSTON.
ROBERTS BROTHERS.
1873.

CONTENTS.

TITLE AND CHARACTER
OF THIS BOOK.

THIS Volume of Discourses, chosen with care from
the mass of Channing's manuscripts, is named THE
PERFECT LIFE, because the Title best marks its
Character. It is now published, as apparently
called for by the wide reception of his writings,
and in the assurance that it will meet with welcome
from his large circle of friends in the Old World
and the New.

In reading these Discourses it should be kept
constantly in mind, that they are precisely what
they claim to be—a Minister's pulpit addresses
to his own Congregation. They are neither Lectures for the learned, nor Essays for a literary
circle, nor Papers for a critical Journal. Still
less are they a Theological Treatise. But they are
Calls to the People to "come up higher." In them

great truths are presented in the most popular form, and brought home to the common heart. Written for delivery, week by week, during the last ten years of Channing's life, it was manifestly his purpose to adapt his lessons to the apprehension of his simplest hearers. He would have all to share in the bright prospects, which had shone before him in hours of solitary thought and devout communion. And knowing that he was often charged with yielding to the charms of an ideal exaltation, that secluded him from the work-day world, he wished by cordial hospitality to make the humblest his peers. Thus reverent friendliness pervades the tenor of these appeals. And sublime sincerity inspires their style.

It was Channing's wont, season by season, on his return to his pulpit in the autumn, to lay freely open the regions of truth, which he had been exploring during his summer holiday. And almost invariably his winter's sermons fell into Series. In these "Twelve Discourses on The Perfect Life," then, we may imagine this earnest Preacher as engaged in interpreting his Ideal Philosophy for his People's use. In clear terms, terse phrases, compact sentences, and frequent though varied re-statements, he bears his listeners, by easy transitions upward, from the level plain of average experience to the loftiest summits of speculation. And on those serene heights, above the discordant din of theological controversy and worldly strife, he welcomes all to worship the Father face to face, and thence look down in hope upon the widespread promise of Peace on earth, imaging the harmony of Heaven.

Let us trace the movement of Channing's mind, as he thus leads the procession of his followers :—

I. The first discourse is initiatory in its definitions, general statements, and broad survey of the route to be traversed. At outset, "The Religious Principle in Human Nature" is defined as the Love of the *Perfect*, that for ever aspires towards relationship with the ALL-PERFECT ONE. And the affirmation is announced as an Axiom, that the End of human existence is PERFECTION; which can be attained only by entering into living communion with The Living God.

II. In the second discourse, the revelations of the Infinite Being, through His manifestation of Perfection in the Universe and in Humanity, are disclosed. And from the lessons of Wisdom, taught by these Two Witnesses, is drawn the ennobling view, that worship is the ascent of the Soul to its Original,—the Divine in man seeking the Supreme Divinity, — whereby we become transformed into the Goodness, that we adore.

III. The third discourse presents, as the Object for adoration, the Universal Father,—whose Eternal Infinite, Parental Love, flows forth with impartial equity, to every Individual Child throughout His vast Family of All-Souls. And this discourse culminates in a cheerful prediction of "The Better Day," when universal humanity shall melt away partition walls and make of the broad earth one happy home.

IV. The fourth discourse appeals to every heart with the touching truth, that the Creator and Sustainer of the Boundless Universe is the Lover of Persons. And it unfolds, with utmost simplicity, the laws of order,—whereby the Highest Spirits, the Human Race, and Single Souls are indissolubly united by *vital* ties in one immortal organization, which is centred in and embraced by the LIVING Love of the Father of All.

V. In the fifth discourse, from this assurance of God's Parental Interest in Individual Persons is drawn the animating truth, that, frail, finite, mortal, as apparently we are, we may yet utterly confide in the purpose of the All-Perfect to make us partakers of His own Perfection, in an immortal, ever-unfolding career of Boundless Good.

VI. By this survey of the immense sweep of Human Destiny we are taught, in the sixth discourse, to recognize that Life, with all its varied forms of Good, is a free gift from the All-Giver. Channing here unfolds one of his most characteristic and cherished convictions, by declaring that *in addition* to the sustaining energy of the Divine IMMANENCE, we need, for our spiritual growth, to seek and gain the continual aid of the Divine INFLUENCE, through Personal Communion. And in a most eloquent passage this saint reveals to us, how by experience he had learned to *know* the TRANSCENDENT God,—as the Person of Persons, and his Personal Friend,—and so had for ever escaped from the abyss of Pantheism, by filial fellowship.

VII. Gratefully accepting Life, then, as a Gift, in the seventh discourse, the Preacher proceeds to a comprehensive study of the End for which it is given. And he shows, how all tendencies of Human Nature and all events of Human Experience conspire to prove that the *only* End which can satisfy the Soul's boundless longings, and fulfil the Divine Ideal in man, is Spiritual Perfection.

VIII. The eighth discourse developes this Ideal of Spiritual Perfection, under its two highest forms of Moral Rectitude and Intellectual Integrity. The aim of this richly-suggestive discourse is to represent Religion as the universal Quickener and Illuminator. And in the progress of his argument, Channing sketches in outline his conception of The Perfect Life, as a beautiful, harmonious *whole* of healthful, joyous Goodness.

IX. This prepares the way for the ninth discourse,—a Christmas Sermon,—in which Channing pours forth the fulness of his love for Jesus Christ, as the embodiment in Mind, Character and Life of Ideal Perfection. In none of his published writings will be found a more fervent testimony to the humanizing Influence of this well-beloved Brother, Friend and Emancipator. And this discourse closes with an Invocation—the only one found in his manuscripts—to the First-born among many Brethren.

X. From this recognition of the promise of Perfect Life, given to the human race in the spirit and influence of Jesus, in the tenth discourse, the Preacher enters into the inmost Essence of the Christian Religion, and demonstrates conclusively that its central principle is Goodness. With child-like singleness of mind he avows his belief, that neither on earth nor in heaven can a Higher Good be found than Goodness, because it is the Essential LIFE of the All-Good. In conclusion, he illustrates the urgent need of applying this pure, large, free-hearted form of the Christian Religion to the Political and Social movements of our age, throughout all Nations.

XI. Affirming thus, in uncompromising terms, that Jesus can confer no higher salvation than Divine Disinterestedness, and that the Father can welcome us to no sublimer bliss than to a participation of His own Holiness, in his eleventh discourse, Channing ascends above the clouds of dogmatic Theology into the clear, sunny atmosphere of Truth. And there he reveals to us in all its splendour the reality, that Goodness is the very glory of God, indwelling in Humanity and in the Blessed Societies of Heaven.

XII. Finally, in the twelfth discourse, the seer places us upon the topmost peak of his mount of vision. Thence he discloses to us his confident hope, that the Centre of Unity for the Human Race is given, in the Son made One with the

Father, and with the whole Family on Earth and in Heaven, by a Life of LOVING COMMUNION. And his prophecy is crowned with a calm yet triumphant utterance of faith, that the Risen Head of the Church Universal lives evermore to organize his Brethren and Friends into One Perfect Community, amidst the brightening beauty of the Universe and the constant light of the Divine Presence.

When these Discourses are thus read in connexion, it will be seen what a natural order Channing follows in opening his Ideal of The Perfect Life. Yet plain, obvious and direct as they are,—when they were first preached, not a few within Channing's denomination, and his own congregation even, criticized them as "Transcendental." For such hearers could not credit his assertion that man may entirely trust the Revelation of God given in Human Nature,—in conscience, reason, love and will,—in reverence for the sublime and joy in the beautiful,—in the desire for blessedness such as earth cannot appease,—in the Ideal of Perfection,—and above all in the longing for Oneness with the Infinite Being by affinity and fellowship. His bold affirmations, that all minds are of One Family,* that Jesus with his celestial love is the

* Discourse on God revealed in the Universe and Humanity.

Life of his religion,* that his Character is at once the image of Divine Perfection, and the type of man's Spiritual Perfection when grown to fulness of stature, and raised to right relationship of filial and fraternal communion with God and humanity, were deemed "enthusiastic." And his cheering prediction of a New Order of Society, when communities, as well as individuals, will make it their end to realize in deeds this Ideal of Perfection, was condemned as the spiritual "romance of a visionary."†

But the seasons have moved forward in the grand year meanwhile. And now this fore-runner of the Better Day‡ has found fit audience among the spiritually-minded and saintly, the free-thoughted and earnest of many communions, ——among scholars, statesmen and economists of his own and other lands,—among philanthropists, educators, social reformers and the people of all Christian nations,—and finally, among the seekers after purer faith and humaner manners under the "Ethnic Religions."§

The materializing tendencies of Natural Science,

* Discourse on Jesus Christ the Brother, Friend and Saviour.
† Introduction to his Works, 1841.
‡ Discourse on the Universal Father.
§ James Freeman Clarke's "Ten Great Religions."

as taught in various schools to-day, bring out by
contrast the significance of Channing's Idealism;
for it is seen that his doctrine of pure Theism is
their needed counterpoise. His positive faith in a
Personal God, with whom every Spirit must seek
living intercourse, in the attainment of personal
integrity, is found by experience to be the vital
cure for the paralyzing fatalism, that deadens heroic
action in so many modern Pantheistic Schemes.
His reverence, blended with dignified self-trust, and
devoutness sanctifying courage, help to form the
grand style of character, that can alone insure the
calmness, wisdom, equipoise and energy, called for
in times so unstable. And his great-hearted
humanity, honouring humble and high impartially,
as born to be peers on earth in the Father's
Family, and co-heirs in the glory of Heaven, is
recognized as the very temper fitted to balance
loyalty with freedom, and equity with progress, in
our transition age. Finally, the Goodness, which
he so glorifies as the Essence and End of the
Religious Life, and as the very manifestation of
God in Humanity, is approved by the experience
of ages to be the sole true Bond of Unity among
the Children of the Universal Father. Indeed
each change that succeeds in scientific speculation,

religious development and social reform, throughout the Commonwealth of Christendom, but serves
to show how well adapted Channing's Gospel is to
the Present Age,* alike in its aspirations and its
doubts, its enterprises and its conflicts, its tantal-
izing failures and its resistless growth.

Channing's own Spirit and his Practical Aim
will be found revealed in this volume, more freely
even than in his preceding works. The same
"great ideas" everywhere re-appear indeed, for
they "formed the man;" and by them, according
to his wish, "he will be judged."† But in these
discourses they come forth with vivid freshness, and
even youthful exuberance of expression. And
by combining in order, as has been briefly done,
the views presented of "THE PERFECT LIFE,"
from its germ in "The Religious Principle in
Human Nature" to its full development in
"Heavenly Society," a quite complete conception
can be framed of his Theory of Human Destiny. That he prized these discourses, as em-
bodying his ripe convictions, is proved by the
fact that they were delivered in many pulpits,
and that several of them were copied under his

* Lecture on "The Present Age."
† Introduction to his Works, 1841.

own eye with the intent of publication. And, doubtless, a volume like the present one would have appeared, if his ministry had not been cut short, just when he felt that a wider sphere of usefulness was opening. No one knew better than Channing did himself, however, that the truths, which he so cherished, were premature. And so keenly alive was he to this unseasonableness, that it was his constant aim, as a Preacher, by frequent iteration of a few central principles, by measured under-statement of sublime doctrines, by toning down his predictions of man's probable development to familiar phraseology and thought, and, in a word, by continually translating his poetry into prose, to justify to Common Sense his Ideal.

For those, indeed, who had the ear to hear the undertone, that thrilled through his spoken words, and the eye to read the underlying meaning of his published Works, and his Memoir, it must have been long since manifest, how much more was implied than was declared. He gave but fragments of his Theodicy, Ethics and Polity, and was patiently waiting for health and leisure to unfold them fully.* Yet though conscious of the critical scep-

* His proposed work on " Man."

ticism and apathy pervading his era, his trust was steadfast, that the Laws of Life, of which he was a herald, would quicken in due time all communities. And never was he so buoyant, glad and young, as during the last summer of his earthly course. His sunset was serene with the hope of a To-morrow soon to dawn,—of Filial Worship, uniting the Good of all names and nations into One Church Universal,*—of Social Co-operation in labour, property, culture, binding the various classes of every nation in Fraternal Fellowship,— and of Peace made permanent by a concert of beneficent action around the globe.† His spirit was all aglow with the coming of an age of righteousness and love, wherein by religious reverence for every Person as a Child of God, by generous Interchange of all kinds of good, and by a joyful consciousness of the Divine Indwelling in Humanity, a Heaven on Earth shall be really organized in Law and Life. This ardent trust found utterance in his last address at Lenox, August 1, 1842, which so unexpectedly proved to be his parting benediction to his Race.

The circulation of Channing's Works, wherever

* Sermon on "The Church Universal."
† Discourses and Lectures on "War," etc.

the English Language is used, and their translation among the leading Continental Nations, insures a wide reception for this volume. But even in presence of the hearty response given to his appeals for "Reverence to Human Nature," by advanced thinkers in Europe and America, it may be questioned whether his compeers have even yet fairly measured his *characteristic* claims. The very simplicity of his style leads readers to underrate the scope of his spiritual vision. Majestic principles stand forth so clearly through the medium of his transparent thought, that their distance, height and range are seldom justly gauged. Hereafter, probably, he will be found to have been a more sagacious Seer, alike for nations as for individuals, than even his devoted disciples anticipate. And only after transformations in the Science of Theology, in the Ideals of Personal Greatness, and the Ferms of Human Society, which he foresaw and foretold, will this Prophet of Universal Humanity be honoured at his full worth.

Such is the confidence with which this volume is offered to the increasing company of Channing's friends. Its editor has sought to make it a faithful Portrait of the Man, as he *lived*, in the inner circle of Home, and among his own People. And if he may define in briefest terms the quality by which these Discourses are characterized, and for which after-comers will hold them dear, this quality is: The Purity, Largeness and Loftiness of their RELIGIOUS LIFE. One central principle, as we have seen, animates them all:—that the End of man's being is to be Perfect, as the Father in Heaven is Perfect. And this principle of Perfection is applied, in its fulness, to every relation, duty and interest, personal, communal, national and humane. As a second trait, these Discourses are inspired by a wisdom, that admirably balances and blends earnest faith with fearlessly free inquiry, piety almost enraptured, though never mystical, with sound judgment and sober good sense, scrupulously high-toned ethics with fervent liberalism in social and political reforms, and poetic enthusiasm with practical sagacity and impartial justice. And finally, they are tempered in tone by an unassuming dignity, greatness of heart, and urbane graciousness, which prove in what a rare degree his grand Ideal of the Perfect Life had become a Real Person in the harmonious character of CHANNING. .

W. H. C.

As for God, His way is perfect. God is my strength and power: and He maketh my way perfect.—2 SAMUEL xxii. 31, 33.

Mark the perfect man, and behold the upright: for the end of that man is peace.—PSALM xxxvii. 37.

I will behave myself wisely in a perfect way. O when wilt Thou come unto me? I will walk within my house with a perfect heart.—PSALM ci. 2.

I have seen an end of all perfection: but Thy commandment is exceeding broad.—PSALM cxix. 96.

Be ye therefore perfect, even as your Father which is in Heaven is perfect.—MATTHEW v. 48.

Perfect in one.—JOHN xvii. 23.

I.

THE RELIGIOUS PRINCIPLE

IN HUMAN NATURE.

THE RELIGIOUS PRINCIPLE
IN HUMAN NATURE.

———

The Lord our God is one Lord: and thou shalt love the Lord thy God with all thy heart, and with all thy soul, and with all thy mind, and with all thy strength: this is the first commandment.
—MARK xii. 29, 30.

———

THE command thus given to love God with all the heart, and soul, and mind, and strength, is in harmony with our whole nature. We are made for God; all our affections, sensibilities, faculties, and energies are designed to be directed towards God; the end of our existence is fellowship with God. He could not require us to devote our entire being to Himself, if He had not endowed it with powers which fit us for such devotion. Religion then has its germs in our Nature, and its development is entrusted to our own care. Such is the truth that I would now illustrate.

I.—The Principle in Human Nature, from which religion springs, is the desire to *establish relations* with a BEING more PERFECT than itself. The fact is as remarkable, as it is incontrovertible, that the human race, all but universally, has conceived of

some Existence more exalted than man.   If there is
one principle, indeed, that may be declared to be
essential in human nature, it is this unwillingness to
shut itself up within its own limits, this tendency to
aspire after intercourse with some Divinity.   It is
true that men at various periods have formed most
unworthy conceptions of their objects of worship.
Still, by selecting the qualities which they esteemed
most highly in themselves, and by enlarging and
exalting them without bounds, they have shown,
as plainly as have more enlightened ages, the spontaneous longing of the human spirit to rise above
itself, and to ally its destiny with a Supreme Power.

This simple view is sufficient to prove the grandeur
of the Religious Principle.   Without doubt, it is the
noblest working of Human Nature.   In the most
immature manifestation of this principle, we behold
the budding of those spiritual powers, by which, in
the progress of the race, men have attained to the
conception of Unbounded Goodness.   We see this
principle in the creations of genius, in forms of ideal
beauty to which poetry and the arts give immortality, in fictions where characters are portrayed
surpassing the attainments of real life.   We see this
principle in the admiration with which stupendous
intellect and heroic virtue are hailed, and in the
delight with which we follow in history the career
of men who in energy and disinterestedness have
outstripped their fellows.   The desire for an ex-

cellence never actually reached by humanity, the aspiration toward that Ideal which we express by the word PERFECTION, this is the seminal principle of religion. And this is the root of all progress in the human race. Religion is not an exclusive impulse. It does not grow from an emotion that is centred wholly upon God and seeks no other object. It springs from the same desire for whatever is more Perfect than our own nature and our present life, which has impelled man towards all his great spiritual acquisitions and to all great improvements of society. This principle, as we have seen, prompts the mind to create imaginary beings, and to attach itself with delight to human agents of surpassing power and goodness. But in these objects it can find no rest. These are too frail a support for so sublime an emotion. This principle God implanted for Himself. Through this the human mind corresponds to the Supreme Divinity. This principle, being in its very essence insatiable, partakes of the nature of infinity; and no Being but the Infinite One can supply its wants.

This view conducts us to an important standard, by which to judge of the Truth and Purity of any form of religion. A religion is true, in proportion to the clearness with which it makes manifest the Perfection of God. The purity of a particular system is to be measured by the conception which it inspires of God. Does it raise our thoughts to a

Perfect Being? Does it exalt us far above our own nature? Does it introduce us to a grand and glorious Intelligence? Does it expand our minds with venerable and generous conceptions of the Author of existence? I know no other test of a true and pure religion but this. Religion has no excellence, but as it lifts us up into communion with a Nature higher and holier than our own. It is the office of religion to offer the soul an Object for its noblest faculties and affections, a Being through whom it may more surely and vigorously be carried forward to its own perfection. In proportion then as a religion casts clouds around the glory of God, or detracts from the loveliness and grandeur of His character, it is devoid of dignity, and tends to depress the mind.

All human systems are necessarily defective. They partake of the limits of the human mind. The purest religion which man ever has adopted, or ever will adopt, must fall very far below the glory of its Object. Our best conceptions of God are undoubtedly mixed with much error. We talk indeed of Truth, as if we held it in its fulness; but in religion, as elsewhere, we make approaches only to the Truth. We see God in the mirror of our own minds; but these are narrow and in many ways darkened. We see Him in His works; but of these we comprehend a minute portion only. He speaks to us by His spirit in scripture and in the heart; but He speaks to us in human language, and adapts Himself to our weak capacities, so that we catch mere glimpses of His perfection. The Religious Principle itself, by which we perceive and love God, is as limited at birth as are our other faculties, and is gradually unfolded. It embraces error at first by necessity. The earliest idea of God in the child is as faint as are its conceptions of all other objects. Necessarily it invests the Creator with a human form, places Him in the heavens, and clothes Him with an undefined power superior only to that possessed by those around it. This idea however of some Being higher than man takes root; and from this religion grows up. As we advance, we throw off more and more our childish notions, purify our thought of God, divest Him of matter, conceive of Him as mind, refine away from Him our passions, and especially assign to Him the attributes which our growing consciences recognize as righteous and holy. Still we are making approaches only, and slow approaches, towards God. Much of earth, much of our own incompleteness, still clings to our conception of the Divinity whom we worship. And the wise man is distinguished by detecting continually whatever is low in his apprehension of God, and by casting it away for more exalted views.

II.—I now proceed to show more directly that religion is natural to man and is his great end. And for this purpose I go to Human Nature. Time will permit but few illustrations of this great theme; for when we survey man's various faculties, affections, and powers, all concur in bearing testimony to the truth now advanced. All are but so many elements of religion.

1. Look first at the Reason, that divine germ within. I ask you to consider what are the primitive, profoundest, and clearest ideas of Reason. They are the very ideas which lead to God. The earliest inquiry of Reason is into Causes. Even the child breaks his toys to discover the spring of their motion. Reason cannot satisfy itself with observing what exists, but seeks to explore its origin. It asks by instinct, whence comes the order of the universe, and cannot rest until it has ascended to a First Cause. The idea of God is thus involved in the primitive and most universal idea of Reason, and is one of its central principles.

Among other tendencies in the Reason to God, one is especially noteworthy. I refer to its desire for comprehensive and connected views. The Reason is never satisfied with beholding objects separately. By its very nature it is impelled to compare them with one another, to discover their similar or diverse properties, to trace their relations, their respective fitnesses, and their common bearing. And it never rejoices more than when it attains to some great Law, which all things obey, and by which all are bound together. Through this principle we have learned that the sun, earth, and planets, form a connected whole, and obey one law called attraction; and still more we have risen to the sublime conviction, that all the heavenly bodies, countless as they may be, are linked together by mutual dependencies and beneficent influences into one system. Now this tendency to search for connexion and harmony —for Unity—in the infinite variety of nature, is a direct tendency to a belief in One God. For this unity of nature manifestly proves, and can only be explained by, unity of thought, design, and intelligent power; that is, it proclaims One Omnipotent, All-comprehending Creator.

2. Look next at the Conscience; and here we see another natural tendency to religion. What particularly strikes us in this principle of our nature, is that it not only enjoins the law of duty, but intimates that there is a Ruler above us, by whom this Law will be sustained and executed. Conscience speaks not as a solitary, independent guide, but as the delegate of a higher Legislator. Its convictions of right and wrong are accompanied with the idea of an Authority more awful than man's, by which these distinctions will be enforced. That this is the natural suggestion of Conscience we learn from the fact that men in different ages, countries and conditions, have so generally agreed in speaking of the inward monitor as the voice of the Divinity. In approving or condemning ourselves, we do not feel

as if we alone are the judges, but we have a presentiment of standing before another tribunal. Especially when we see the wrong-doer prosperous, do we feel as if the injustice of fortune ought to be redressed. We demand an Almighty Patron of virtue. Retribution is the claim of our moral nature. So powerful is this tendency of Conscience to assert a righteous Deity, that we cannot escape the sense of His Presence. Often when the guilty have tried to efface the impression of a Supreme Lawgiver, the commanding truth has defied their power. The handwriting of the Divinity in the soul, though seemingly obliterated, has come out with awful distinctness in the solemn seasons of life. Thus Conscience is a prophet of religion. And in proportion as it is obeyed, and the idea of Right becomes real and living within us, the existence of the Almighty Friend of virtue is intimately felt, and with profoundest reverence.

3. If we pass next to the Affections, we shall recognize still more clearly that our nature is formed for religion. What is the first affection awakened in the human heart? It is filial love, a grateful sense of parental kindness. And is not this the seed and prime principle of religion? For what is religion but filial love rising to our Father in heaven? Thus the first emotion of the human heart is virtually towards God. Its first spontaneous impulse is an element of piety.

Another characteristic emotion of our nature is that feeling of Approbation, with which we look on disinterested benevolence. We cannot conceive of a human being quite wanting in this moral principle, whose heart would not expand at witnessing in a fellow-man philanthropy unaffected, unwearied, and diffusing happiness far and wide. Here is another germ of religion. For what is religion but sympathetic joy in the unbounded beneficence of God? what but this very affection of esteem raised to Him who is the source of all good-will in men, and before whose glory of disinterested love all other goodness is but a shadow?

I proceed to another affection of our nature which bears strong testimony to our being born for religion. I refer to the emotion which leads us to revere what is higher than ourselves, to wonder at the incomprehensible, to admire the vast, to adore the majestic. There is in human nature an affinity with what is mighty, an awful delight in what is sublime. It is this emotion which draws man to the grandest scenes of nature, to the wilderness and ocean, to thundering cataracts, and the still solemn mountain top. It is manifested in the interest which the multitude take in persons of commanding intellectual energy, of heroic courage, of all-sacrificing devotion to the cause of freedom and humanity. Men are attracted by no quality so much as by sovereign greatness of will. They love whatever bears the impress of the infinite. So strong is this principle of Reverence, that when fallen from the knowledge of the true God, they have sought substitutes in their own teeming imagination, have deified fellow-men, have invented beings in whom they might concentrate and embody their conceptions, just or unjust, of Supreme dignity. Thus the heart was made for worship, and worship it will. It longs for something more excellent than it finds on earth. In works of poetry and fiction it continually creates for itself a more than human glory. This emotion of Reverence is a perpetual impulse in the soul towards God.

Another emotion of our nature, and closely related to reverence, next claims regard, as a germ of religion. This is the love of the beautiful. Beauty, that mysterious charm which is spread over and through the universe, who is unconscious of its winning attraction? Whose heart has not softened into joy, as he has looked on hill and valley and cultivated plain, on stream and forest, on the rising or setting sun, on the constant stars and the serene sky? Now whenever this love of the beautiful unfolds into strong emotion, its natural influence is to lead up our minds to contemplate a brighter Beauty than is revealed in creation. To them, who have eyes to see and hearts to feel the loveliness of nature, it speaks of a higher, holier, Presence. They hear God in its solemn harmonies, they behold Him in its fresh verdure, fair forms, and sunny hues. To great numbers, I am persuaded, the beauty of nature is a more affecting testimony to God than even its wise contrivance. For this beauty of the universe is an emblem and revelation of the Divinity, and the love of it is given to guide us to the All-Beautiful.

Thus we see that human nature is impelled by affections of gratitude, esteem, veneration, joy, not to mention various others, which prepare us to be touched and penetrated by the infinite goodness of ·God, and which, when directed to Him, constitute piety. That these emotions are designed to be devoted peculiarly to the Creator, we learn from the fact that they are boundless in their range and demand an Unbounded Object. They cannot satisfy themselves with the degrees of love, intelligence, and power which are found in human beings. They excite the imagination to conceive of higher, richer, ampler excellence than exists on earth. They delight in the infinite, and never can they find repose but in an Infinite Being, who combines all good.

4. I might easily multiply views of human nature, all tending to show that religion is natural to man. But I will add only that the human soul has two central motive principles, which are specially fitted to raise it to God. There is in all human beings an insatiable desire for Happiness, which can never be appeased in our present existence, which the universe is wholly inadequate to gratify, which becomes only

more intense amidst life's sufferings and disappoint-
ments, and which is only deepened, expanded, and
purified by our highest experience of joy. And
there is in refined minds a still profounder and more
urgent impulse, already indicated, the longing for
Perfection, for deliverance from all evil, for perpetual
progress, the desire to realize in character that bright
Ideal of which all noble souls conceive. These aspirations appear wherever men are found, now in sighs
and lamentations, now in struggles and ardent efforts.
But there is no good on earth that can fulfil their
claims. They require an Infinite Blessedness and
Perfection; and innumerable weary spirits have they
led up to God.

5. Thus have I endeavoured to show, by a few
illustrations, that all the great principles of human
nature are germs of religion, as impulses towards
God. If further proof were needed of its congeniality
with our nature, I would appeal to facts. Let us ask
History then whether religion be natural to men.
What principle has acted with equal energy on
human affairs? To what principle did all ancient
legislators appeal as the foundation of civil institutions? To religion. What principle was it that
gave Mohammed the Empire of the East? What
principle under the Crusades precipitated Europe
into Asia? I grant that these movements arose out
of excesses of the religious principle. But we learn
by its excesses how deeply planted are its roots in

our nature. And in the largest historic view, what principle is it that has produced in all times and lands the most devoted and fearless martyrs, that has sung hymns of praise in the depths of dungeons, that has smiled with hope on the scaffold, endured without a groan the rack and fire, and refused to accept deliverance when one recanting word would have set the sufferer free? O, the miraculous power of the religious principle in the human soul! How has it led men to forsake the cheerful haunts of their fellow-beings, and to live in solitary cells, that in silence they might open their hearts to God and feel His joy-inspiring presence! What has it not strengthened men to do and to suffer! What speechless sorrows has it not soothed! What strength, peace, hope, has it not breathed into the dying! Yet it is a question whether our nature was formed for religion! The strongest love which the human heart has ever felt has been that for its Heavenly Parent. Was it not then constituted for this love? Where but in God can it find an Object for its overflowing fulness, of reverence and affection, of aspiration and hope?

III.—My friends, we all possess indeed this capacity for religion. Let us not wrong it by neglect. It is, as we have seen, the central and all-pervading principle of Human Nature. And by proper means it may be cultivated, expanded, and made supreme. To give it life and vigour should be our highest aim.

Here is the great field for our activity. By turning our chief energies abroad, we frustrate the end, and defraud ourselves of the proper happiness of our being. The world within is our great domain, worth infinitely more than the world without. To enthrone God in our inmost being is an immeasurably grander aim than to dispose of all outward realms. We boast of the power which we are daily gaining over material nature, how we bend the elements—fire, wind, steam—to our uses; and we look with compassion, if not scorn, on ages when man did not dream of this dominion. But may not a more fatal ignorance be found among ourselves? There is a loftier power of which we seldom adequately conceive. It is man's power to combine and direct the spiritual elements of his being, his power to free the intellect from prejudice and open it to the influx of Truth, his power to disengage the heart from degrading selfishness and to commune with God by disinterested love. This power we all possess, and we should prize it more than life.

By this language I do not mean that we are to exalt our religious character by ourselves alone. I am not so unwise as to claim for men any independent strength. The truth is we cannot learn a science, art, or language, without aid. It is only by help from other minds that we improve our own, or achieve any important enterprise. It is only by help from the mineral world and the elements that we cultivate the land or traverse the sea. And without God's perpetual sustenance we could do absolutely nothing, and should not even exist. I am not teaching man's isolated energy. His power consists in ability to seek and use assistance from nature and from his fellow-creatures. Above all it consists in ability to seek and to use Spiritual Influence from God. This Influence may be gained by aspiration and by effort. It is in truth constantly exerted upon us, even when unsought,— exerted in every dictate, encouragement, warning, reproof of conscience and reason, in every secret longing of the soul for freedom from error and evil and for growth in wisdom and virtue. Aids without measure are offered to us by God. And when I say that love towards God is placed within our reach, I mean that it is so placed by the Inspiration which He incessantly pours on every human being.

What might we not become, were we but just to ourselves and to the means of religious life thus bountifully afforded from heaven! We have all, I trust, a faith in God, and occasionally recognize our near relation to Him. But we can attain to more than cold belief, to more than formal worship, or to transient emotions of gratitude. The religious principle may become the very Life of our souls. God, now so distant, and perhaps little more than a name, may become to us the nearest and most real of all beings. We may cherish a reverence and attachment to

Him more profound and devoted, than the affections with which we embrace parent, and child, and dearest human friends.   And through this strength of piety we may gain an immovable strength of moral principle, an unbounded philanthropy and a peace which passeth knowledge.   This capacity for religion is a spring. of perennial freshness in every human breast.   I would not resign it for the gift of count-less worlds.   It invites us to Him from whom, as a living centre, all suns and systems with their beauty and blessedness shine forth, and of whose glory they are but the dim reflex.   We pity the barbarian, in whom intellect and imagination and sensibility slumber.   But do not diviner capacities slumber in many of us?   Gifted with the power of honouring God and of living with Him in filial intimacy, do we not desert Him and bury our souls in transient cares, distinctions, gains, amusements?   Let us re-tire into ourselves, and become conscious of our own nature and of its high destination.   Let us not profanely debase or destroy it.   There is an inward suicide more awful than the destruction of the animal life, an inward ruin more mournful than any wrought by the conflagration of cities, or the desolation of whirlwinds.   The saddest spectacle in this or in any world is a rational and moral being, smitten with spiritual death, alive only to what is material and earthly, living without God and without hope.   Beware of this inward death—this insensibility to the Presence, the Authority, the Goodness of our Heavenly Father.

Do you ask by what means this end of entering into living communion with God can be attained? I answer first: Let us each put forth our best force of Intellect in gaining clearer and brighter conceptions of the Divine Being. We must consecrate our loftiest powers of thought to this sublime Reality. We must not leave to others the duty of thinking for us. We must not be contented to look through others' eyes. We must exercise our own minds with concentrated and continuous energy. One chief source of truth for us, in regard to God, is Revelation ; and this, accordingly, should claim our most serious and devoted study. But when I thus speak of Revelation, I mean the Christian Religion. In the Jewish Scriptures, though many sublime passages are found in relation to the Supreme Divinity, yet in many others the image given of God is adapted to a rude state of society only, and to a very immature stage of the human mind. And not a few Christians have depressed their idea of the Infinite Being, by conceiving of Him as He was represented in half-barbarous ages, instead of learning to know Him from Jesus, who came to scatter. the shades of Judaism as well as of Heathenism, and who alone reveals the Father—or the Paternal Character of the Creator—in full glory. Again, in studying the Christian Revelation, we must take our views of God from what is clear rather than what is obscure, from the simple teachings of Jesus, rather than from the dark reasonings in some parts of the Epistles. Still more we are to learn the Divine Character in Christianity, not merely from passages which expressly describe Him, but from the character of Jesus Christ, who came to be an image of the Father, and also from the character which Jesus seeks to form in us—that is, from the precepts of this religion; for these are intended to exalt us into the likeness of God. Whoever combines these three sources of knowledge—the express declarations concerning God—the virtues manifested in Jesus Christ —and the virtues which he inculcates,—whoever looks to these, for the Character of the Supreme Being, cannot misapprehend its grand features. I have said that our best force of Intellect is to be employed on Revelation. But Revelation is not the only source of spiritual light. The great design of Jesus Christ is to teach us to see God everywhere, in Nature, in Providence, and in the Human Soul. He perpetually points to God's works for instruction, and to His manifestations through humanity. And we cannot comprehend Him aright, if we do not go beyond Revelation, and take lessons in religion from all that we observe, enjoy and suffer. Jesus came, not to shut us up in a Book, but to open the Universe as our School of spiritual education.

But in teaching you to use the Intellect faithfully and independently in acquiring just views of God, I have given the least important precept. With this we must join obedience to God's Will, so far as we know it, or all intellectual effort will avail us little. We may indeed by study, or by living among enlightened people, acquire a just theory in regard to our Creator. But it will be Theory only. It will be a knowledge of words more than of realities,—a vague superficial apprehension,—unless the mind prepare itself by purifying obedience for an intimate knowledge of God. Moral discipline is much more important than a merely intellectual one, for gaining just apprehensions of the Supreme Being. I beg you to consider this. To know God we must have within ourselves something congenial to Him. No outward light, not the teachings of hosts of angels, could give a bad man bright conceptions of God. A man who yields himself up to selfish ambition, to avarice, to sensuality or to sloth, who sears his conscience and hardens his heart, is as effectually shutting his mind on the All-Good, as he would deprive himself of the light of the sun by deadening the optic nerve or by destroying the structure of the eye. Intellectual learning helps a man not a step towards God, unless conjoined with inward spiritual discipline—government of the passions, reverence for conscience, and growing development of good principles and affections within. The Infinite Spirit must be revealed to

us in the unfolding and operation of our own
Spirits, or we shall never truly know Him. For
example, God's Purity, or aversion to sin, may be
read and talked of, but is never understood, until
conscience within us is encouraged to reprove all
forms of evil. The solemn and tender reproof of this
inward monitor alone enables us to know the moral
displeasure of the righteous Lawgiver, in whose
name and with whose authority it speaks. In the
same manner we have a superficial knowledge only
of God's Goodness, we know nothing of it intimately,
until a Spirit of Love, bearing some resemblance to
His own, springs up within ; until, through some con-
quest over the selfish principle, virtuous benevolence
begins its work in our minds. This it is that helps
us to comprehend the Father, to recognize and respond to that Love, which shines forth from every
region of creation. Again, every man who has read
the New Testament knows how it teaches that the
mind is God's great work, and that it is destined to
an immortal existence. But the mere reading of
this in a book gives us no conception of the reality.
Unless my own spirit makes progress in truth and
virtue, and so reveals to me a measure of its power
and beauty, I may hear about Immortality, but I
shall receive little more than a sound. Nothing
external can tell me what a glorious principle the
Mind is. The sublimest work of the Creative Mind
will be hidden from me. And having in my own

heart nothing which speaks of the Immortal Life, that doctrine will be but a word on my lips. I appeal to you all for a confirmation of this. I ask you whether thousands under the bright light of Christianity are not almost as ignorant, as the heathen, of the true God. Do not a few commonplaces or trite expressions, about His greatness, goodness and mercy, uttered in a manner which show that their meaning is not felt, make up their stock of knowledge on the sublimest realities? No outward teaching can bring us to a vision of the Divine Being. The soul must join with intellectual effort a moral operation upon itself. And Christianity contributes to our knowledge of God, by nothing more than by setting this truth before us, by awakening a consciousness of our infirmities, and by inciting us to obey the conscience in its remonstrances against sin, and its monitions to duty.

Would you then attain to the love of God with all the heart, and soul, and mind, and strength, begin with purifying yourself from all known evil. Let your fervent prayer be to Him to animate you in your conflict with bad passions and habits, and in steadfast obedience to His Will. With this purifying purpose of obedience, read the Scriptures; and the simple passages, in which Jesus speaks of his Father, will open on your minds with new brightness. In this temper study the character of Jesus; and in him, who was the image of the Father, you will learn

to see more and more distinctly the fulness and free-
ness of Divine Benevolence. In this spirit of obedience look on nature, and observe the works of the
Creator, and their beauty and harmony will become
more touching, till gradually heaven and earth will
grow eloquent in their Author's praise. In this
spirit look into your own minds, observe what is
good and great in the minds of others, and the Infinite Mind will more and more appear to you in His
crowning creation, the human soul. And finally,
with this purifying purpose of duty, pray for the
Divine Spirit, and you will receive it. A secret
Influence will aid your efforts after oneness with
the Holy One. Peace, silent as dew, will distil on
you from heaven. I believe too, that with such a
temper and life, you may enjoy something more
than distant communications from the Father of
Spirits; that you may be favoured with those blessed
seasons of universal light and strength, of which
good men have often spoken, in which the mind
seems warmed by a new flame, and quickened by
a new energy from on high, and which, though not
miraculous, still bring with them a near consciousness of the Divine Original, and come like the very
Breath of God upon the soul. Through these
various methods, you will ascend by degrees to a
living communion with our Creator, which, however
low compared with what awaits you in another life,
will yet be lofty in contrast with all you could

have conceived of, in the beginning of your religious course.

I close with re-affirming the truth that I have aimed to impress. Religion is not an unnatural or unattainable good. Its germs exist in us all. We have, each of us, the spiritual eye to see, the mind to know, the heart to love, the will to obey God. We have a Spiritual Nature that may bear the image of Divine Perfection. Glorious privilege! Let us not cast it away. Let us not waste our souls on perishable objects. For these souls may become Temples for indwelling Divinity. They may even partake of the glory and the blessedness of the Living God. May we all, through a just exercise of intellect, and a sincere and purifying obedience, enjoy this gradual illumination and sanctification, which are the beginning of Heaven! You will then learn how cold is the most earnest language of the preacher, and how inadequately the loftiest human eloquence can unfold the blessedness of a spirit making progress towards fellowship with the All-Perfect One.

II.

GOD REVEALED IN THE UNIVERSE AND IN HUMANITY.

GOD REVEALED IN THE UNIVERSE AND IN HUMANITY.

Doth not Wisdom cry? and Understanding put forth her voice? . . . Unto you, O Men, I call; and my voice is to the sons of Man.— PROVERBS viii. 1–4.

THE passage from which these words are taken is designed to teach that the Truth, which can guide us to Perfection and to Happiness, is teaching us always and everywhere; that God surrounds us constantly with His instruction; that wherever we go the voice of His Wisdom follows us; that it is our own fault if we are not continually becoming wiser and better. This universal presence of Truth is the subject to which I ask your attention. To understand this will help us to understand our whole existence. For it will show us that under every lot we have exhaustless means of growth. And thus it will awaken us to new faithfulness in the use of our privileges, and to new efforts in the pursuit of Goodness.

Wisdom is omnipresent. Everywhere it comes to meet us. It shines in the sun. It irradiates the heavens. It whispers through all sounds of nature. It beams resplendent from the characters of good and wise men, and more brightly still in our own souls. Our teachers are thus all around and within, above and beneath. Divine Wisdom is not shut up within any book. It is not heard from pulpits alone. It has better preachers than all ministers. And one great aim of the true minister is to help his hearers to understand wiser teachers than himself, and to open their ears to more harmonious voices. By turning their minds to the lessons of every day, he should make them feel that they are in a higher than any human school,—in God's own School, the School of the Universe,—where always and everywhere they may be gathering treasures of Truth.

Jesus said: "I am the Light of the World." And when did he say this? At the moment when he was about to open the eyes of the blind man. To that man he was to be a light. And how? By creating a new light for him? No! The light existed already. The sun was shining on him then in unclouded splendour. A thin membrane was the sole barrier between that blind man and the glorious world which lay around on every side. By lifting this veil Jesus gave him light. In a similar way Jesus Christ is a light to us spiritually. He creates no new truth; for Truth is eternal. And what is still more important, he does not teach truth wholly new to men. The great principles of religion belong to Human Nature ; and they are manifested in all God's Works and in His Providence. We live in darkness, not because there is no Sun of Truth shining on and around us. For a spiritual light, brighter than that of noon, pervades our daily life. The cause of our not seeing is in ourselves. The inward eye is diseased or shut. Were that but opened, we should at once be introduced into a Spiritual Universe, fairer and more magnificent than the Creation which burst on the eye of the blind man, when Jesus said : " Receive thy sight."

Wisdom is omnipresent. The greatest truths meet us at every turn. Jesus came to reveal the Father. But is God, the Infinite and Universal Father, made known only by a single voice, heard ages ago on the banks of the Jordan, or by the sea of Tiberias? Is it an unknown tongue that the heavens and earth for ever utter ? Is nature's page a blank ? Does the human soul report nothing of its Creator ? Does conscience announce no Authority higher than its own ? Does reason discern no trace of an Intelligence, that it cannot comprehend, and yet of which it is itself a ray ? Does the heart find in the circuits of creation no Friend worthy of trust and love ? O, yes ! God is on every side, not only by His essential invisible Presence, but by His manifestations of Power and Perfection. We fail to see Him, not from want of light, but from want of spiritual vision.

The same remark may be extended to Jesus' doctrine of Immortality, though with limitation. The future world indeed is in no way laid open to the senses. But the idea of it is one of the most universally recognized among men. The thought of Immortal Life preceded Jesus. We meet glimmerings of it even in the darkest and most barbarous times. The germ of this great truth is in our Nature; in the Conscience, that includes as one of its elements a presentiment of retribution; in the Reason, that beholds in the present an incomplete destiny, needing to be continued for the fulfilment of its end; in the thirst for Happiness, that is too deep to be satisfied on earth, but opens into aspiration towards an infinitely Blessed Being; in the love of moral goodness and beauty, which in proportion as it is cultivated awakens the Ideal of spotless virtue and a desire of community with the All-Perfect One. The voice of our whole nature indeed, properly interpreted, is a cry after higher existence. The restless activity of life is but a pressing forward towards a fulness of good not to be found on earth, and indicates our destination for a state more brightly beautiful than we can now conceive. Heaven is in truth revealed to us, in every pure affection of the human heart, and in every wise and beneficent action, that uplifts the soul in adoration and gratitude. For Heaven is only purity, wisdom, benevolence, joy, peace, in their perfected form. Thus the

Immortal Life may be said to surround us perpetually. Some beams of its glory shine upon us in
whatever is lovely, heroic and virtuously happy in
ourselves or in others. The pure mind carries
Heaven within itself, and manifests that Heaven to
all around.

In saying that the great truths of religion are
shining all about and within us, I am not question-
ing the worth of the Christian Revelation. The Christian Religion concentrates the truth diffused through
the universe, and pours it upon the mind with solar
lustre. Still more it heals our blindness by exposing
the passions and sins, which veil the mind against the
light of the Spirit, and furnishing the means to
remove the films, which gather over the inward eye
and prevent us from seeing the revelations of Nature.
We cannot find language to express the worth of
the illumination thus given through Jesus Christ.
But we shall err greatly, if we imagine that his
Gospel is the only light, that every ray comes to
us from a single Book, that no splendours issue
from God's Works and Providence, that we have no
teacher in religion but the few pages bound up in our
Bibles. Jesus Christ came, not only to give us his
peculiar teaching, but to introduce us to the imperishable lessons which God for ever furnishes in our own
and all Human Experience, and in the laws and
movements of the Universe. He intends, not that
we should hear his voice alone, but that we should

open our ears to the countless voices of wisdom, virtue, piety, which now in whispers, now in thunders, issue from the whole of Nature and of Life. He does not give us a narrow system, and command us to bound inquiry within its limits. He does not prison reason by a rigid, formal creed. He gives us generous Principles, which we are to carry out and apply everywhere, and by which we are to interpret all existence. He who studies nothing but the Bible, does not study that book aright. For were it rightly read, it would send him for instruction to every creature that God hath made, and to every event wherein God is acting. That reader has not read aright the Sermon on the Mount, who has not learned to read sermons in the changes of the seasons and in the changes of human history. Wisdom spoke through Jesus as her Chief Oracle. She beamed forth from the life and lessons of this Divine Saviour, with the pure unsullied glory in which she manifests herself in Heaven. But Wisdom does not confine herself to one shrine. Her light is not bounded to a single orb. To the humblest that calls she gives her responses. We live amidst a host of teachers of moral and religious truth. Unsought, unpaid, they beset our path. Rejected they still plead. They begin their ministry with our first breath; and they do not forsake us in the last hour.

In these remarks I have again and again referred to Two Great Teachers, which are always giving us lessons of Wisdom: 1st, The Outward Universe; and 2nd, The World of Thinking, Moral Beings. My chief purpose in this discourse is to direct you to the voice of Wisdom that issues from Humanity. But the Revelation of God through Nature shall be briefly considered first.

I.—The voice of Wisdom—that is of Moral and Religious Truth—speaks to us from the Universe. What a blessing would it be to us, one and all, could we but really wake up to the glory of this Creation, in which we live! Most men are actually asleep for their lifetime in this vast and magnificent world. Mighty changes are going on around them, fitted to entrance their souls in wonder and thankfulness; and yet they are moved no more than if they were shut up in a mill, seeing only the perpetual revolution of spindles, and hearing only the monotonous hum and clatter of machinery. We might have been born amidst such machinery, had the Creator so pleased. And men's insensibility often seems to deserve no better lot. But instead of being pent within narrow walls, we live amidst this immeasurable Universe. Instead of a few pale lamps giving only necessary rays, oceans of light daily overflow this planet whereon we dwell, with inexhaustible splendour and beauty. And the fire that sustains the life of earth's creatures is for ever freshly kindled millions of miles away.

If I should be called to express in a word the most

important lesson that Wisdom utters in the Creation,
I should say it is this. Nature everywhere testifies to
the Infinity of its Author. It bears throughout the
impress of the Infinite. It proclaims a Perfection
illimitable, unsearchable, transcending all thought
and utterance. It is modelled and moulded, as a
whole and in its least molecule, with grandeur, unfathomable intelligence, and inexhaustible bounty.
This is the glory of the Universe. And to behold
this is to understand the Universe. Until thus we
see the Infinite in Nature, we have not learned the
lesson that Wisdom is everywhere teaching. I say
that the Infinite is revealed in all things. I do not
except the most common. The stone falls to the
ground by a force that controls the sun, the planets,
and all worlds throughout immensity. Did not the
dropping apple reveal to Newton that the very law,
which brought that fruit to the ground, keeps the
earth in its orbit, and binds creation into one harmonious whole? Behold the humblest wild flower. To
produce that weed all Nature has conspired. Into
itself it receives the influence of all the elements—
light, heat, and air. Sun, earth, and ocean meet to
pay it tribute. The least thing in nature acts upon
all things, and is acted on by all; so that each implies all and is represented in all. In a word, to
understand the simplest work of God, the Universe
must be comprehended. For that work, however
frail and transient, could not exist, did not all things.

else exist. It is a living part of this mighty living Universe. It has innumerable ties with the limitless Creation—connexions too subtle, swift, and ever-changing, for any finite mind to trace. Thus each minutest particle speaks of the Infinite One, and utters the divinest truth which can be declared on earth or in heaven.

Again, there is an impenetrable Mystery in every action and force of the Universe, that envelopes our daily existence with wonder and makes sublime the familiar processes of the commonest arts. How astonishingly does Nature differ in her modes of production from the works of human skill. In a machine of man's making we can trace the motive power, and detect the arrangement whereby this power is transferred from part to part. But in Nature, so vibrating with motion, where is the Moving Energy? Can you discern the all-embracing, all-pervading Force that gives the primal impulse to the moving whole, and perpetuates movement through immensity; that wheels planets and suns in their vast orbits, and at the same instant quickens countless and multiform animals and plants? Look at a grain of wheat! That seed is the fruit of all harvests of past ages since the creation of the world. It carries us back to the hour when the morning stars sang for joy over the new-born earth. In it are centred the combined forces of suns and rains, of soils and climates, for a period of which history has no record.

And again, this tiny seed has within it prolific energy to cover whole kingdoms, it may be the whole globe, with vegetation, and to multiply itself without end. On such mysteries as these the science of ages has shed little or no light. And they open a deeper mystery still. What and whence is that principle called Life, to which this seed owes its distinctive organic character,—which can modify and counteract the laws of nature, which can mould the plant to symmetric wholeness and unfold it into consummate beauty? Life, that awful power, so endlessly various in the forms it assumes,—Life that fills earth, air, and sea with motion, growth, activity, and joy,— Life that enlivens us, what is it? What sight can discern, what thought explore its mystery? Thus the Infinite, the Mysterious, the Unsearchable meets us, veiled in the lowliest creations. But that which falls within the range of our senses is as nothing compared with the invisible, the intangible, the incomprehensible, that lies beneath. And if Wisdom thus speaks through the minutest existence, what a voice comes to us from the Immensity, wherein we are encompassed!

What blessedness it is to dwell amidst this transparent air, which the eye can pierce without limit, amidst these floods of pure, soft, cheering light, under this immeasurable arch of heaven, and in sight of these countless stars! An Infinite Universe is each moment opened to our view. And this Universe is the sign and symbol of Infinite Power, Intelligence, Purity, Bliss, and Love. It is a pledge from the Living God of boundless and endless communications of happiness, truth and virtue. Thus are we always in contact, if I may so say, with the Infinite, as comprehended, penetrated, and quickened by it. What unutterable import is there in the teachings of such a Revelation! What a Name is written all through it in characters of celestial light! A Spiritual Voice pervades it, more solemn, sublime and thrilling,. than if the roar of oceans, thunders, whirlwinds and conflagrations were concentrated in one burst of praise. This voice is all the more eloquent because it is spiritual; because it is the voice in which the All-Wise speaks to all Intelligences.

II.—This leads us to consider the voice of Wisdom that utters itself from the Spiritual World, the world of moral and intelligent beings, the Humanity of which we each form a part. This topic is immense. For the book of Human Nature has no end. New pages are added to it every day through successive generations. The moral and religious truths, which Wisdom may draw from the human soul, from human life, from human experience, cannot be exhausted. From these I shall select one great lesson only, which all history attests. This lesson is that there is in human nature an element truly Divine, and worthy of all reverence; that the Infinite which is mirrored in the outward Universe is yet more brightly imaged in the inward Spiritual World; or, in other words, that man has powers and principles, predicting a destiny to which no bound can be prescribed, which are full of mystery, and even more incomprehensible than those revealed through the material creation.

That this is the lesson uttered continually by Wisdom through what we see familiarly in human life, is a doctrine that may startle some, who think that observation leads to very opposite results. To many persons, history and experience seem to warrant no feelings higher than pity or contempt for their race. The error of these observers should be traced to two sources: first, they do not understand the highest office of Wisdom; secondly, they rest in a half-wisdom which is worse than ignorance. To each of these errors a few words may. be given.

1. They who disparage Human Nature, do so from ignorance of one of the highest offices of Wisdom. The chief work of Wisdom consists in the interpretation of Signs. To know what is present and visible merely is to know nothing. The great aim should be to discern what the visible present signifies, what it foreshows, what is to spring from it, what is wrapped up in it as a germ. Wisdom sees the future in the present, for it sees in the present the signs of that future. This actual world may be defined as a world of Signs. What we see

is but the sign of what is unseen. Beneath the properties, which meet the eye, lie others incomparably more potent. In life an event is the prophetic sign and forerunner of other coming events; and its importance almost always consists, not in its own independent character, but in the tendencies and influences which are wrapped up in it, in the future good or ill of which it is the harbinger. These remarks peculiarly apply to Human Nature. For of this it may be said that we know hardly anything but signs. It has merely begun its development. It has taken the first step only in an endless career. Its best emblem is the seed just shooting above the surface of the earth, and struggling to disclose its folded petals. That, which man has as yet felt and thought and done, is a foretoken only of what he is to feel and think and do. The worth of his best attainment lies in what it prepares for. The present stage in Man's history, studied without reference to his future, would lead to endless error. For his highest improvement is but a hint and faint foreshadow of his destination.

2. The second consideration, by which may be explained the common erroneous estimate of Human Nature, is that most men rest in a half-wisdom, which is worse than ignorance. They who speak most contemptuously of man tell the truth, but only half the truth. The wounds and sores of human nature, which they delight to expose, are real. In condemning

human crimes they invent nothing, they exaggerate
nothing.   History and experience do testify to a widespread taint of selfishness and injustice in our Race.
They, who assert the greatness of human nature, do
not differ on this point from its vituperators. They do
not bandage their eyes. They see as much of guilt
as the man of worldly wisdom.   But here lies
the difference between them and the worldly wise.
Amidst the passions and selfishness of men they see
another element—a Divine element, a Spiritual Principle.   They see powers and affections always struggling against evil in the human heart, which are
celestial in their nature, and which speak of an immortal destiny. In these they discern the true interpretation of Human Nature, in its origin and its end.

Let us avoid half-wisdom. It is the root of the
most fatal prejudice. We wrong individuals not so
much by falsely ascribing to them defects, as by
taking one-sided views of their characters as a whole.
And in the same way we wrong our Race. I am willing to concede to the man of worldly wisdom all his
charges against existing society. I will go farther,
and tell him that he does not comprehend the depths
of actual evil.   For to do this requires a moral
sensibility to which he has not attained. I have no
eulogies to pronounce on the present condition of
human nature, in even the most civilized communities.
Our whole social fabric needs thorough, searching
complete reform. But I do not stop here. If I did,

.I should lose the great lesson that Wisdom proclaims from every page of history. This lesson is, that Man, with all his errors, is a wonderful being, endowed with incomprehensible grandeur, worthy of his own incessant vigilance and care, worthy to be visited with Infinite Love from Heaven. The Infinite is imaged in him more visibly than in the outward Universe. This is the great truth to be learned from all our social combinations. This is the germ of all confident and joyful effort for human improvement. It is the very root of Free Institutions. From it alone can spring high-toned moral relations and happy intercourse between men. This truth is the central principle of Christianity, and from failure to recognize this, our existing systems of education, policy, legislation and social intercourse, are poor, narrow and impotent. So great a truth is this, which I affirm as being taught from the whole of Man's social life. I know with what incredulity I shall be heard, when thus asserting that the only lesson, worth learning from society, is the one which as yet has been learned least. And unhappily false theology has joined with low worldliness in barring men's minds against its reception. But it is not less true, nor less important, because doubted and denied. Man really is a mysterious being, endowed with divine powers and welcomed by a boundless destiny. Such is the truth. And I hold it all the faster for the incredulity of theologians and men of the world.

Having thus combated the disparaging views so prevalent in regard to Human Nature, and having showed their origin, and proved that the very circumstances, which give them birth, if justly interpreted, are sufficient to refute them, I shall next aim to exhibit directly the testimony of human life to the Divine in Man.

The subject is so large, that it is best to fix attention on a single point. And I go at once to the most common, though the sublimest principle of man,—the Moral Principle. What is so common as the idea of Right ? Where do we not meet with its presence, in all relations of human life,—in all systems of education, in our legislative halls, our historic memorials, our courts of justice, our tribunals of public opinion, our familiar conversation, our private friendships, our humane and religious organizations ? The whole of human life is indeed a recognition in some way or other of moral distinctions. And no nation has existed, in any age, that has not caught a glimpse at least of the great principles of right and wrong.

The Right, the Just, the Good, the Holy—these words express an excellence, that awakens in us emotions of reverence and esteem, altogether distinct from the impulses we feel towards other forms of Good. Conscience, in enjoining duty, reveals to us its supreme worth. The Right is higher altogether in its essential quality than the profitable, the agreeable, the graceful. It is that which must be done though all other things be left undone, that which must be gained though all else be lost. Other kinds of Good are valued in consequence of their adaptation to our peculiar constitution. But Justice, Goodness and Right deserve to be valued for their own sake. It is conceivable that we might have been so framed as to prefer darkness to light, or to find nourishment in what is now poisonous. But a being so constituted as to see baseness in disinterested love and venerableness in malignity, would be an inconceivable monster. In truth we can no more imagine such a moral being, than we can imagine an intelligent being who could think of a part as being greater than the whole. To perceive the Right then is to recognize the Supreme Good, that which is worthy of supreme love, that which not only solicits us by promises of enjoyment, but utters the voice of absolute command and claims sovereign dominion. How sublime then is this principle of Right, and how great the Mind of which it is an element!

Every human being I have said has this idea of Right. This is not all. He has not only the idea of Right; but he himself is capable of Rectitude. We are made not only to admire the Right; for the same faculty, that discerns it as a Universal Law, proclaims it to be our own Supreme Law. Right is not revealed to us as the glory of unapproachable beings, whom we must reverence at a hopeless distance. It is made known to us with the consciousness, that rectitude is bound up with our own lives. This we all feel. No experience is more familiar. And yet nothing more substantially great can be said of the Highest Being in the universe. Is there one among us who has never made a sacrifice to duty, never denied a passion, never foregone a pleasure, never borne a pain, rather than violate the inward law of Right? The power of resisting evil exists in every man, whether he will exercise it or not. The power of clinging to the Good, the Just, the Holy, amidst trial and loss,—we all possess it. And we know that we have it; for we are conscious of our degradation when we fail to use it. This power, so continually put forth by us all against inferior temptations, is a germ which may be expanded into a divine energy. In some men this celestial might is actually unfolded. And to them we should look, with grateful admiration and affectionate homage, as the true revelations of Human Nature. There have been men, in whom the Right, the Good, the Holy, have awakened all-conquering love; in whose spirits high moral excellence, such as was manifested in Jesus Christ, has shone with a brightness above the sun; who have concentrated the whole strength of their nature into the resolve of well-doing; who have grasped and held fast duty with a deliberate energy, which has grown in proportion to the powers arrayed against it; who could not be separated from the Right by tribulation and distress, by persecution or famine, by the rack or the sword. These are the heroes of human history, who give effulgence to the records of the past. Such heroism, though rare, is not superhuman. It is the expansion, the developed form only, of that very power, which every man puts forth, when he makes the slightest sacrifice to duty. This high rectitude exists as a seed in every heart. It is indeed the very essence of humanity.

In the preceding remarks, I have spoken of the principle of Right in the human heart, as revealing duty to the Individual. I now proceed to another view, which has all along been implied, but which deserves distinct exposition. You perceive what is Right and Good, and feel yourself bound to respect it. But is this all? Does duty reveal itself as a personal obligation merely, or as confined to yourself? Is a rule made known, by which you alone are to walk? When justice, goodness, truth, purity, are urged on you by conscience, is there not a distinct conviction that these are not a merely personal obligation? Do you not at once recognize that a Law of Right is promulgated within you, to which *all* men are subject? Still more, do you not feel that this great Law of Right binds not only men, but ALL Intelligent Beings; that it is the law not of the earth only, but of the Universe? Does the Right seem to you a transient, arbitrary ordinance, which may hereafter be repealed, and to which other beings and men may be strangers? Have you not, on the contrary, an intimate conviction that the Right is as everlasting, as it is universal? Justice, goodness, disinterestedness, truth, purity, love, do you not transport these ideas to Heaven? Are they not in fact the essential elements of your conception of Heaven? Is it not through them that you imagine beings in higher stages of existence? Is not the very idea of a higher being this, that the elements of Moral Perfection dwell in him in fulness and unity, as they are not unfolded upon earth? Here then we learn the greatness of Human Nature. This moral principle—the Supreme Law in man—is the Law of the Universe—the very Law to which the highest beings are subject, and in obeying which they find their elevation and their joy. Then man and the highest beings are essentially of One Order. They form One Family. The same Spirit of Goodness enlivens all. To all there is the same Supreme Law, the same Supreme Good! Imagination and genius, in their most inspired moments, can picture nothing in heaven brighter than Moral Goodness— that very Goodness, of which the germ unfolds in the humblest human heart. This Goodness is seen by us intuitively to be confined to no place, to no time, to be the growth of no nation and of no world, but to be universal, eternal, immutable, absolute, and worthy of highest veneration and love by All Spirits, for-ever. Can we then look on the human soul, which is at once the oracle and the subject of this Universal and Eternal Law, as created only for time and this narrow earth?

As yet, we have but approached the true greatness of Human Nature. We come now to views of the Soul which thrill us with transport, for the utterance of which all language is feeble, and towards which all thought is but a faint approximation. Man, though human by nature, is capable of conceiving the Idea of God, of entering into strong, close, tender and purifying relations with God, and even of participating in God's Perfection and Happiness. We hear this great truth unmoved. It is a truth to wake the dead! It ought to exalt our whole life into joy. What I have thus far said is but a preparation for this. I have spoken of the principle of the Right, the Good, the Holy. But without this Idea of God—the PERFECT BEING—the moral principle would pine and die in its conflict with evil. I have spoken of the unbounded tendencies and aspirations of this principle; but without an Infinite Father for their object and support, such aspirations would be vain yearnings, and would soon give room to despair. This moral nature within us, so alive to the Right, is still weak and imperfect, needing to be nourished, fortified and fulfilled by communion with Supreme Excellence. It needs a Perfect Being for its love, an Almighty Being for its trust, an Everlasting Being under whose unchangeable aid it may unfold for ever. It cannot live and move without faith in the Righteous Governor of the universe, who will repress wrong and reward well-doing with the best of all recompenses, growing strength in highest virtue.   Thus the moral nature of man feels after, and must find God.   The reason, why men see God in the outward creation, is that their own Nature has an affinity with Him, and cannot be unfolded or find repose without Him.   We comprehend and desire Him, because we carry His image in our Moral and Intellectual Powers, and because these tend to their Source.   Is there nothing great then in Human Nature ?   Within it is wrapped up this Idea of God ; it is carried to Him by inward impulses and wants.   It sees in the outward creation God's Omnipotence.   But it hears in its own conscience the voice of God's Authority.   It feels itself vitally related to God, not merely like matter by physical dependence, but by a moral law.   It has a consciousness of accountableness to Him, which in its degradation even it cannot throw off.   It can reverence God, and still more it can love Him.   Is there no grandeur in such a Nature ?   There can be no higher Idea in the universe than this of God. There can be no greatness like that of adoring Him, of harmony with His Goodness, of concord with His Will.   This adoration, this concord are not only within man's power, but they are the very end of his being; and in no other destiny can we find rest and joy.

It is true that the Idea of God has been mournfully obscured by human passions. Still amidst the ruins of man's religious nature some celestial fire has slumbered. And particularly interesting is it to observe, how the consciousness of some divine element in human nature has mingled with the grossest superstition. Thus we witness, widely spread among heathen nations, the practice of deifying distinguished men—legislators, patriots, heroes. But why were the greatest and best on earth believed to be raised to heaven? Because the illustrious of the race were thought to be of the same family with the gods. There was gross superstition in this worship offered to the dead. But beneath that error, as beneath most errors, lay a great truth. In that widespread practice, the *affinity* between God and Man was dimly shadowed forth. Therein appeared that truth, which has since shone out so brightly in the union of the Human and the Divine, in the Character of Jesus Christ. How sublimely great is Man, when thus regarded as a Spiritual Being in fellowship with the Infinite Spirit! Within him is enshrined the Idea of God. He calls God his Father.

And now it may be asked, what are the practical uses of these views? I answer, the greatest of all truths are the most quickening. And to nothing so much as to the obscurity, that eclipses them, is the low standard of the Christian World to be traced.

Again is it asked, why I am so anxious to declare these views of human nature now? I answer, I prize these views because they confirm my faith in Jesus Christ, and give reality to the great hope that Christianity sets before us. Jesus came, as he taught us, to create men after the likeness of God, to breathe into men a divine virtue, and to prepare them for the heavenly life. The sceptic derides this good as unreal, because wanting in adaptation to our nature. But I look into human nature and cannot but feel that a being made for such a destiny, as Christianity reveals, must carry within him tokens presignifying his end. It is a joyful confirmation of my faith, then, to find in the human soul plain signatures of a Divine Principle, to find faculties allied to the attributes of God, faculties beginning to unfold into God's image, and presages of an immortal life.

Another practical use of the views now given of human nature is this. In proportion as they are received, they will transform essentially our modes of relationship, communication, and association with our fellow-beings. They will exalt us into a New Social Life. Indeed they will give an entirely new character to social intercourse. That intercourse must be determined by the estimate we form of human nature. He, who looks on man as little better than a brute, will live with men as brutes. He will be wanting in reverence for their rights and feelings. He will think only of making them his instruments. He will be anxious chiefly to raise himself above them by outward distinctions. He will care little how they are trampled under foot. He will scoff at the thought of living and dying for their happiness. Society is now degraded through all its laws, institutions, and customs, by the blindness of men to the Divine Principle within themselves and one another. Once diffuse this great truth through society, and it will work a mightier revolution than politicians ever dreamed of. It will ennoble all social duties. It will give sanctity to all social relations. It will breathe a deference and tender respect through manners, which will put to shame what now passes for courtesy. It will bring an end to that outward, ostentatious, superficial life, on which so many squander time, means, thought and their best powers. It will awaken an intense effort for distressed humanity. It will send far and wide a spirit of reform, from the nursery to the hall of legislation. It will substitute the holy tie of Human Brotherhood for all artificial bonds of social order. With this great truth in his heart a man cannot insult a fellow-man, for he beholds the Divine in the Human. He can call no being low in whom his own highest powers and affections are wrapped up. Can you conceive then of a truth so practical as this doctrine of the greatness of man as a moral being? It will create a New Earth.

And, finally, to speak of its highest use, how would

this doctrine, brought home to the heart, transform our fellowship with God! Time is wanting to unfold this great subject now. It has never as yet been fitly unfolded. For want of an enlightened conviction of man's participation in a Divine Principle, religion in all ages has sunk more or less into superstition. It has bowed down the spirits which it ought to have uplifted. It has been deemed a means of propitiating a Higher Power, instead of being regarded as the ascent of the Soul to its Original, as the Divine in man seeking the Supreme Divinity, as a homage changing us into the Goodness we adore, and strengthening our disinterested love of fellow-beings with a Celestial Life. How earnestly to be desired is it, that religion should be thus raised from selfish superstition into generous Communion with God. And never can it attain to this its true glory, till man shall better comprehend himself as a Child of God, and the filial relationship, inherent in his very nature, between himself and the Father of Spirits.

My friends, how little do we know ourselves! How unjust are we to ourselves! We study everything else but the Divine Principle within our own Persons. The truth may be on our lips. But in how few hearts does it live! We need a New Revelation—not of Heaven or of Hell—but of the SPIRIT within ourselves.

III.

THE UNIVERSAL FATHER.

THE UNIVERSAL FATHER.

Is He the God of the Jews only? Is He not also of the Gentiles?
Yes, of the Gentiles also.—ROMANS iii. 29.

THE writings of the Apostle Paul have met with a singular fate. They were intended to reveal the Father's universal and impartial love; and they have been used to represent Him as an exclusive and arbitrary Sovereign. They were designed to open the Kingdom of God to all men; and they have been so distorted as to shut it on the many and confine it to the few. They breathe the most liberal spirit; and yet from them have been drawn the main arguments for intolerant bigotry. Nothing stranger ever happened in the history of human thought. From Paul, the grand teacher of Divine Grace and Mercy, who lived to break down the barriers between Jew and Gentile, and to unite the Human Race in brotherly love, have been derived the mournful dogmas—that God elects a certain number to salvation, and dooms the rest to everlasting woe; that the reception of an unintelligible creed is essential to man's redemption, and that they who hold this are authorized to denounce all who reject it, as enemies of God and as unworthy of a place in the Church of Christ.

From the history of Paul's Epistles, we learn how fatal it is to substitute the letter for the spirit of Divine Revelation, and how dangerous it is to read the Scriptures, without carrying into their interpretation our Reason, and the light of Conscience. They have not been studied with the common intelligence and candour, which men carry to the perusal of other writings. And hence the free, bold language of the Apostle has been perverted from its original significance and made to support a system, which reason and conscience revolt from, and which transforms Christianity from the Gospel of glad tidings into the saddest message ever preached.

The great design of Paul's Epistles was to vindicate the spiritual right of the Human Race against the exclusive bigotry of the Jews; to manifest God as the Father of all men, and to teach that He did not shut Himself up in the land of Judea or the temple of Jerusalem; that Jesus Christ came to save not one narrow nation but the whole world; that the Kingdom of Heaven, the infinite blessings of the Gospel, were opened with boundless freedom to Humanity universally. This is the great "Mystery," or in other words the long-hidden purpose of God, of which Paul speaks in such magnificent language. By this "Mystery" he meant no unintelligible dogma, but God's merciful design, concealed from the ages, "to gather together in One" the whole Human Family under Jesus Christ, to break down all divisions between nations and classes, and to unite men of every kindred and condition in one Spiritual Worship of the Universal Father. Take with you this great truth, and you have the key to Paul's writings. Without it, the rich treasures of that noble teacher will be a sealed book.

In our text we have the central idea of Paul's Epistles. I shall first offer some remarks on the doctrine that God is "the God of the Gentiles," chiefly to strengthen our convictions of its truth; then, in the second place, I shall consider the universal principle contained in this doctrine; and thirdly I shall apply this principle to our times and our own moral needs.

I.—God is "the God of the Gentiles." To understand the full import of this sentence of Paul, we ought to consider the circumstances under which he wrote it. This proposition, which in our own days seems too trite to draw attention, manifested at that time an admirable generosity of soul. To the Jew, the Gentiles were odious. He thought it pollution to eat with them. He called them dogs. He was brought up in an antipathy towards the heathen world, for which we can find no parallel. He claimed God as exclusively his God. In all the sufferings of his people he was consoled by their peculiar relation to

the Divine Being, by their supreme religious exaltation above the rest of mankind.　And he lived in
the hope of a swift coming day, in which the
Messiah was to avenge their wrongs, and to bow all
nations at their feet.　For a Jew to renounce this
deeply-rooted and almost ineradicable pride, to come
down from his height of vain-glory and take his
stand among the despised and execrated Gentiles, to
embrace them as brothers and assert their equal
claim to God's love and the blessings of the Messiah's
kingdom—this was an inward revolution, a triumph
over passion, prejudice and education, such as we
now can hardly estimate.　Could we fully comprehend it, we should be filled with admiration for the
moral grandeur manifested in the simple words of
our text.　Paul, in writing them, not only offered
violence to all his earliest and deepest impressions,
but put his life in peril.　Such was the shock
given by his language to the pride and passion of
his people, that they thirsted for his blood, and
wherever he travelled pursued him with murderous
intent.　So stirring were the words which we read
with little emotion. I begin, as proposed, with offering a few remarks upon this doctrine, for the end of
deepening our conviction of its truth.

1. God is "the God of the Gentiles," says Paul;
and do we not respond to this truth? The heathen
nations had indeed wandered far from God; and to
the Jews He seemed to have forsaken them utterly,

But it was not so. The Universal Father was
always in the deepest sense their God. How could
He forsake the millions of His creatures spread over
the face of the earth? Judea was but a speck on
the globe. Its temple was a point too small to be
caught by the eye of the spectator, but a few miles
off. Was the Infinite One to be confined to this
narrow space? Could His love be stinted to the
few, to whom He had specially revealed his Will?
In the very darkest ages God was "the God of
the Gentiles." Though unknown, He was always
near and never ceased to work within them. The
heathen had their Revelation. Light from Heaven
descended into their souls. They had the Divine
Law "written in their hearts." God shone within
them under the ideas of justice, goodness, and duty.
No nation has been found, however sunk and degraded, on which these lights have not dawned.
The rudest savage discerns some distinction between
right and wrong, the just and the unjust, the selfish
and the kind. In every human soul there is a voice
that whispers of the right, a reprover that strikes
awe and awakens compunction, a prophet and judge
that points, however indistinctly, to final retribution,
a conscience that, however resisted, cannot be wholly
silenced. In the rudest tribes we find some recognition of a Higher Power, some glimpse of a Future
Life. And in all these ideas we see God working
in the soul, for its redemption. Nor must we doubt

that in the most corrupt nations He has met with
loving homage and obedience, on which He has
looked with parental favour. The Father has had
many a temple in hearts which never knew his
name. God keep us from the horrible thought, that
the myriads who are buried in heathen darkness are
outcasts from His love! Their spiritual wants should
indeed move our compassion; and the higher light
is given us that we may send it to these brethren.
But Brethren they still are. And they share largely
and freely, as we do, in the love of the Father.
Never does He leave Himself without a witness.

2. That God is "the God of the Gentiles," we
learn from the wonderful progress which human
nature made in heathen ages. Remember Greece—
that land of heroes, poets, sages! God's gift of
Genius—one form of Inspiration — was showered
down on that small territory, as on no other region
under heaven. To Greece was given the Revelation
of Beauty, which has conferred upon her literature
and works of art an imperishable charm, and made
them, next to the Holy Scriptures, the most precious
legacy of past ages. In that wonderful country we
meet not only genius and triumphs of the intellect,
but amidst degrading vices were manifested sublimest virtues. Socrates, choosing to die rather than
refrain from declaring the truth which God had
given him for his people, was a type of the grand
victim to truth and humanity, who in Palestine was

to enlighten and save future ages. Undoubtedly, Grecian philosophy was an imperfect intellectual guide, and impotent as a moral teacher. It often confounded God and Nature, speculated about immortality rather than believed it, and in some schools rushed into utter scepticism. Above all, it had no quickening voice for the mass of men. It gleamed on a few high peaks, and left the peopled valleys without a ray. But was not God the God of the Gentiles, when He awakened in the Greeks such noble faculties of reason, impelled them to such grand works of art, and by their patriotic heroism and peerless genius carried so far forward the Education of the Human Race?

3. God is "the God of the Gentiles;" and He was so just when He seemed to have forsaken them, by separating from them His chosen people. For why was the Jew set apart from the rest of mankind? Why was the broad line drawn between him and the other children of men? From a spirit of favouritism? From partiality to one family above all others? So dreamed the Jew. But nothing was further from the truth. The grand purpose of Providence, in bestowing special spiritual favour on this people, was to prepare the way for the communication of an infinite good to the Human Race. Abraham was called that in his seed all families of the earth might be blessed. Moses was the pioneer of Jesus. Judaism was a normal school to train up

teachers for the whole world. The Hebrew prophet
was inspired to announce an age of universal light,
when the knowledge of God was to cover the earth
as waters cover the sea. Nothing in the history of
the Jewish people shows them to us as God's personal
favourites. On the contrary, their history is a
record of Divine rebukes, threatenings, and punishments. Their very privileges brought on them peculiar woes. Their distinction was a fearful one. In
ages of universal idolatry they were called to hold
forth the light of pure Theism and the worship of
One God. Unequal to this Spirituality, they continually fell from their allegiance, betrayed their
trust, and drew down judgments, terrible as were
ever inflicted upon a nation. At length when the
time came, for which all preceding ages had been
the forerunners,—the time, when the "partition
wall" between the chosen people and the whole
human family was to be prostrated, and the Jews
were to receive the Gentile world into brotherhood,—
they shrank from their glorious task; and rejecting
mankind, they became themselves the rejected of
God. Their past distinction served but as the oc-
casion for their ruin, by the proud and exclusive
spirit that it had roused. Their temple, which
they had refused to open to the nations, sank into
a heap of ruins. And for ages they have been a
scattered, despised, hated, spoiled, and persecuted
tribe. Meanwhile, faith in the One True God, of

which they were unconscious heralds and prophets, has been spread far and wide throughout the Gentile world. Thus we see, that in the very act of selecting the Jew, the Universal Father was proving Himself to be the God of the heathen, even when he seemed to reject them ?

4. This doctrine of God's love to His heathen off-spring is one which we Christians still need to learn. For we too are apt, like the Jew, to exalt ourselves above our less favoured brethren. It is the doctrine of the mass of Christians even now, that the heathen are the objects of God's wrath. All who live and die beyond the sound of the Gospel, it is thought, are doomed to endless perdition. On this ground indeed it is that most missionary enterprises rest. We are called upon to send the Gospel where it is not preached, because men conceive that beyond the borders of Christendom God is an implacable Judge; because no other parts of the earth are believed to hold communication with Heaven; because it is feared that the human being, whose fate it is to be born a heathen, carries to the grave an inherited curse, that will never be repealed. Well do I remember the shock once received from reading a missionary address, in which the speaker computed the thousands of the heathen world who would die during the few hours of the meeting; and he asked his hearers to listen in thought to their shrieks as they descended into hell. But how can a sane man

credit, for an instant, that the vastly greater portion of the human race is abandoned by God? If Christianity did actually thus represent the Character of God, we might well ask what right we have to hold or to diffuse such a religion. For among all the false gods of Heathenism can one be found more unrighteous and more cruel than the Deity, whom such a system offers as an object for our worship? But the Christian Religion nowhere teaches this horrible faith. And still more no man in his heart does or can believe such an appalling doctrine. Utter it in words men may; but human nature forbids them to give it inward assent. Were the Christians, who profess it, deliberately to consider what such a doctrine means, and bring it home to themselves as a reality,—could they distinctly once conceive that every hour, by day and night, thousands of their fellow-beings are plunged by the never-ceasing anger of God into an abyss of endless woe,—how could they endure even to exist? They would look on this world as a hell, and long to escape from the sway of its merciless despot. No! The human heart is a far better teacher than these gloomy systems of theology. In its secret depth it believes, what perhaps it dares not put into words, in God's Impartial, Equitable, Universal and Parental Love.

II.—In the second place, I now proceed to declare the doctrine of our text in its most universal form. We read scripture to little profit, if in passages

relating to local or temporary events, we do not
discover Universal Truths, equally applicable to all
places and times. The language of the text admits
of a spiritual translation. It contains an immutable
truth for all ages. This truth is that God loves
equally all human beings, of all ranks, nations, conditions and characters; that the Father has no favourites and makes no selections; that, in His very being,
He is Impartial and Universal Love. This is the
fundamental Truth of the Christian Religion, entering into and glorifying all its other truths. Let us
glance at a few of its evidences, as given in the
Natural and the Spiritual Universe.

1. This grand Truth of God's universal and impartial love is taught clearly in Nature, by all the
works of the Creator. And this testimony is of great
worth. For God's Works are of the same authority
with His Word. These are His Two Voices, which
are and must for ever be perfectly harmonious.
And we should distrust all interpretations of the
Scriptures, which disagree with the truths derived
from the Universe. The Universe teaches that God
is the God of ALL, and not of the few. When you
look through nature, what mark of a partial Deity
can you discover? Does nature teach the favouritism
of her Author? The central truth of the Universe
is, that God governs by general laws, which bear
alike on all beings, and are plainly instituted for the
good of all. We are placed under one equitable

system, which is administered with inflexible impartiality. Not a blessing reaches any one of us but by ordinances, which provide for all fellow-creatures. This glorious sun, does he not send as glad a ray into the hovel as into the palace? Does he not glorify the same spectacle for every eye? The few opulent may monopolize indeed a human artist's works, may inclose his pictures in their galleries, and shut them out from common gaze. But what are the pictures of all artists combined when compared with the majestic beauty of these serene skies, these golden or gloomy clouds, these ample prospects of earth and sea, which Providence paints each day anew with living colours, and spreads out in harmonious proportions before all His children's eyes! Does the rain fall upon a few favoured fields; or does the sap refuse to circulate except through the flowers and trees of a certain tribe? Some men indeed may prosper above their fellows. But it is by turning to account the great laws which are acting for the benefit of others, as well as for themselves. The farmer, who grows the best wheat on the most fertilized soils, owes his success to no partial bounty, but to his study of seeds and composts, and his obedience to those laws of cultivation which all may apply. Nature is impartial in her smiles. She is impartial also in her frowns. Who can escape her tempests, earthquakes, and destructive powers? For whom does she still the raging waves? Young and old,

the good and evil, are wrapped in the same destroying flame, or plunged in the same overwhelming sea.
Age and infirmity spare no privileged class. We
may spend our treasures in rearing walls against
malaria and pestilence. But Providence has no
favourites. Pain, disease and death break through
the barriers of the strong and rich, as well as of the
humble and the poor. Still more do the awful natural catastrophes, which are interpreted by supersti-
tious fear into expressions of peculiar wrath, fall
without distinction. Thus, in a word, the lesson of
the Universe is God's Impartiality. He has One
Law, One Love, for all.

2. I have called nature to testify that God is the
God of all. But outward nature is not God's highest
manifestation. In religion the Universal Father is
revealed as working in the human soul, and as imparting to man His own Spirit. And is this spiritual
agency of God capriciously confined? Are any
human beings excluded from its influence? God's
Spirit, like Himself, knows no bounds. There is no
soul to which He does not speak, no human abode
into which He does not enter with His best gifts.
Especially do the histories of distinguished saints,
philanthropists, and men of genius disprove the
notion of a local or partial agency of God's Spirit.
From the huts of the poor, from the very haunts of
vice, from the stir of active business, as well as from
the stillness of retired life, have come forth the men,

who, replenished with spiritual gifts, have been the
guides, comforters, lights, regenerators of the world.
It was from a fishing boat on the small sea of Galilee
that God's most effectual ministers of universal religion were called. Those humble voices are now
listened to reverently in the schools, churches and
palaces of all civilized Christendom. Nor was this
a singular case. We have here but an illustration
of a Universal Law. We learn from it that God is
working on human souls in all times and places, and
that men in every lot and sphere receive His Inspiration. At this moment we have a striking example
of this fact, in the great reform that is stirring our
whole nation.* Who now are the most awakening
preachers of Temperance in our country ? Not minis-
sters of religion, not they who never ran into excess.
From the very sinks of intemperance, from shops
reeking with vapours of intoxicating drink, has God
raised up witnesses against this vice. Lips, from
which yesterday drunkenness sent forth oaths, like
blasts from hell, now entreat the wanderer to return
to virtue. Bloated countenances, on which excess
once effaced the lines of humanity, are now radiant
with kind sympathies, as they, who but lately were
reeling sots, win back old companions from the way
to ruin and disgraceful death. Is God's Spirit then
confined to the habitations of the refined and re-
spectable, the well-ordered and sober ? Can we not

* The Washington Temperance Movement.

see how He enters the lowest haunts of guilt and shame, and there finds ministers of truth and sanctity ?

III.—Having briefly considered these plain but decisive proofs of God's Impartial and Universal Love, I proceed to make an application of this Principle to ourselves. We do not need the doctrine for the particular purpose for which Paul used it. But other distinctions between men remain, distinctions of outward rank and condition, of nation and colour, of character and culture, on the ground of which men separate themselves from one another. What a strangeness, coldness, reserve, and hardness of heart, what self-exaltation and exclusiveness, grow out of trifling differences, which are designed by God to create mutual dependence, and to bind us more closely to one another! Time will permit me to dwell upon two only of these illustrations now.

1. Let me first ask, is God the Father of the rich only ? Is He not also the Father of the poor ? How incredibly men exaggerate the distinctions of outward condition. The prosperous are prone to feel as if they are of a different race from the destitute. But to the Possessor of Heaven and Earth, to whom the treasures of all worlds belong, how petty must be the highest magnificence and affluence! Does the Infinite Spirit select as His special abode the palace with its splendid saloons, rich tapestries, loaded tables, and blazing lamps ? Does He fly from the hut with its rugged walls and earthen floor, its cry of half-

famished childhood, its wearing cares, and ill-requited
toil ?   On the contrary, if God has a chosen spot on
earth, is it not the humble dwelling of patient, unre-
pining, trustful, virtuous poverty ?   From the dwellings of the downcast, from the stern discipline of
narrow circumstances, how many of earth's noblest
spirits have grown up !   Voices, which have shaken
nations, have in infancy not seldom asked alms.
Men of genius, whose works have filled the earth
with light, have owed their training to the kindness
of strangers, and their early life has been a forlorn
struggle for bare existence.   But why enlarge upon
what countless biographies of the greatest saints,
scholars, poets, statesmen, philanthropists, attest ?
Bring it to a supreme proof.   When God sent His
Beloved Son into the world, did He summon Archi-
tects and Artists to rear for him a splendid palace ?
May we not still learn a lesson. of Divine Wisdom
from the manger at Bethlehem ?   We celebrate this
incident of the Birth of Jesus in our churches.
Poets sing of it.   Painters illustrate it.   But do we
recall it when we meet the beggar in the streets, or
pass the hovel with its patched windows, leaking
roof and smoky walls ?

2. Once more I ask, is God the God of the good
only, or is He not also the God of the wicked ? God
indeed looks, we may believe, with peculiar approval
on the holy, upright, and disinterested.   But He does
not desire spiritual perfection and eternal happiness

for them, more than He does for the most depraved. The Scriptures even seem to represent God as peculiarly interested in the evil. Jesus illustrates God's love to the fallen by the parable of the shepherd, who, having a hundred sheep and losing one, leaves the ninety and nine, to go after that which is lost, and he adds: "There is more joy in Heaven over one sinner that repenteth, than over ninety-nine just persons that need no repentance." The good do not and ought not to absorb God's love. For the evil have within them equal capacities of goodness. In all men lies, however hidden, an infinitely precious germ of love and holiness waiting to be quickened. And to the all-seeing eye this is never lost. It calls forth unutterable love. Yes! God loves the most evil. We in our conceited purity may withdraw from them, may think it pollution to touch them, may say: "Stand off." But God says to his outcast child: "Come near."

Do I speak to those who have escaped gross vice? Bless God for your happiness. Rejoice in the propitious circumstances, which have conspired for your safety. But do not feel as if God were exclusively your God. Set up no insuperable barrier between yourself and the fallen. Even if you are inwardly as well as outwardly pure ; if you are restrained from self-indulgence, not by external motives, such as custom, opinion and interest, but by deep abhorrence of evil, do not imagine yourselves peculiarly favourites of God. Who of us can claim such peculiar favour on the ground of unsullied virtue? How many wavering steps can we retrace in our past lives, how many lapses, how many wanderings, how many falls! Can we remember no critical moments, when what is called chance determined our characters and conduct, when, if opportunity had seconded our will, we too might have joined the outcast? Do you not feel that you owe what you are to the grace of God, which bore with your frequent frailties, to the inward re- proofs of His Spirit, to the warning voice of friends whom His Providence placed around your path, to events which startled you into reflection, to holy thoughts and subduing suggestions, which were breathed upon your soul you knew not whence? Who can review his own history, and fail to ascribe his salvation to the mercy of God? What sincere man does not feel himself bound by a common experi- ence and a common nature to the reform of his race? A truly good man will indeed know that he is good, will practise no deception upon himself, will be con- scious of his progress, and grateful for it. But he will find that he has become what he is by reliance upon God's Infinite Good-will. He will not indulge in a self-exalting persuasion of his superiority. He knows that he has risen by leaning upon a Higher Power than his own. He knows how midst a thou- sand misgivings, in moments of self-reproach and compunction, he was upheld by confidence in that free love of God, which never forsakes the most unworthy. This great truth, that God's parental love extends even to the worthless, is the strength of the good man from the beginning of his conflicts with evil to the end. Through his own victories he learns to hope for like triumphs in the most erring. His virtue, regarded thus as God's work carried on amidst much imperfection, becomes a bond of union with the vicious. His own spiritual history proves to him that there is a vital energy in the human soul, which vice, however it may deaden, cannot destroy. He despairs of none. He commits all to the love of the Universal Father. To him God is not the God of the good only, but also of the evil.

In speaking thus of the tenderness due to the evil, I have no desire to extenuate guilt, or to break down the distinction between virtue and vice. The distinction is real. We must never confound him who acts from principle with one who is enslaved by passion. That false courtesy, which treats all alike, is treachery to God. We ought to look on the base with indignation. But indignation may be blended with an earnest desire to recover the wrong-doer. This union of stern rebuke with tenderness we know to be possible, for we experience it towards our children, relatives and friends, when they go astray. We ought to detest vice, whether in ourselves or in those most dear to us. But as we love ourselves while reproving ourselves most bitterly, so should we love our erring fellow-creatures, whilst we frown upon and firmly oppose their sins. Indeed the only true love for the bad is that which abhors their corruption, and seeks to arouse in them a like abhorrence. Love can pierce the conscience like a two-edged sword. No violence of anger is so awful as the calm rebuke of love. The tenderness, that apologizes for wickedness, is among the worst forms of cruelty. Whilst God looks on the evil with never-failing compassion, and desires their recovery to virtue, He sends appalling judgments on the impenitent. And, in our sphere, we are to feel and to express the same irreconcilable hatred against all wrong-doing. I plead for no sickly lenity towards the fallen in guilt. I would not disarm the judge seated in each man's breast. This inward oracle seldom pronounces too severe a sentence upon crime. We spare ourselves and others too readily. The true tone of indignant virtue is rarely heard in this compromising world. Conscience must never be silenced. Still the most evil are not forsaken by God. He is for ever their Father, and they are His immortal children. For ever He welcomes them to return to their loyalty, that they may become angels of purity and light. This truth let us never forget. No measure of wickedness should estrange us from our fellows or sever the tie of humanity. Never must we harden our hearts against our brethren, however debased. For their repentance and restoration we should earnestly pray and strive, and should rejoice to pour upon them every spiritual aid, encouragement and consolation. Thus have I sought to illustrate by these two applications the Universal and Impartial Love of God.

And now, in closing, let us ask ourselves distinctly, what was the guilt of the Jews, against which the Apostle so earnestly protested? What was it that levelled their temple to the dust, turned Jerusalem into a heap of ruins, and scattered their nation like chaff throughout the earth? It was their proud separation of themselves from their Race. Their crime was their claim to God's exclusive favour, their unwillingness to receive their fellow-men to equal privileges, their denial of God's impartial love to all His children. And will not the same spirit bring the same ruin upon us? Separation of ourselves from our race is spiritual death. It is like cutting off a member from the body; the severed limb must perish. No matter what separates us from our fellows,—whether it be rank, wealth, culture, genius, or even virtue,—if our good qualities or our good deeds cut us off from sympathy with our race, they become our ruin. Nothing is so odious in God's sight as that pride, that presumptuous spirit of distinction, that haughty looking down upon others, which leads men to magnify what is peculiar in their condition, intellect or character, and to erect this into a barrier between themselves and mankind. Jesus detested and condemned no quality in His

countrymen so severely, as he did this separating
pride. Even the grossest excesses of sensuality
shocked him less than the spirit of the Pharisee.
The spirit of the Pharisee still survives in a thousand
forms. It is the spirit that, on the ground of some
special advantage, whether of outward gain or inward acquirement, says to the less privileged : " Stand
apart." Christianity calls upon us to recognize in all
men the same Immortal Principle, the same germ of
Divinity, the same Image of God.

This spirit of Universal Humanity is the very soul
of our religion. As yet its heavenly power is scarcely
felt. Therefore it is that so few of the blessings of
Christianity appear in Christendom. Alas, we lack
humanity. We talk of it, we profess it, but we con-
tradict its essential principles in character and in
life. We rear partition walls of distinction between
ourselves and fellow-beings. We exaggerate petty
differences. We hedge ourselves round with con-
ventional usages. Nor can we, if we would, without
severe struggle, break through these obstructions to
universal love. Our habits, our established modes
of thought and action, the manners and fashions of
society, all hem us in. Unconsciously and perpetually we violate man's highest right, the right to be
regarded and treated as a Child of God. Man's
noblest Relationship is practically denied. The
grand light, in which this tie ought to be viewed,
has hardly even dawned upon us. What a regenera-

tion it will be throughout all society, when men learn fully to believe in their Spiritual Relationship to One Heavenly Father! We hold this truth in words. Who feels its vitalizing power? When brought home as a reality in social life, it will transform the world. Then will the New Heaven and the New Earth be created. Then will our race become a peaceful and blessed Family, a Temple of true Filial Worshippers. All other reforms of society are superficial. Until men's eyes shall be purged to discern in one another, even in the most degraded and fallen, a ray of the Divinity, a reflexion of God's image, a moral and a spiritual nature within which God works, and to which He proffers heavenly grace and immortal life; until they shall thus recognize and reverence the Eternal Father in all His human Children, the true bond of Communion will be wanting, between man and man, and between man and God. Till then, under all forms of law and courtesy will lurk distrust and discord, infusing pride, jealousy and hate into the individual heart, into domestic life, into the intercourse of neighbourhoods, into the policy of nations, and turning this fair earth into the likeness of hell. But a Better Day is coming. The Kingdom of Heaven is at hand. A purer Christianity, however slowly, is to take the place of that which bears but its name. Cannot we become the heralds of this Better Day? Let our hearts bid it welcome! Let our lives reveal its beauty and its power.

IV.

THE FATHER'S LOVE

FOR PERSONS.

THE FATHER'S LOVE
FOR PERSONS.

———

Even the very hairs of your head are all numbered.—LUKE xii. 7.

———

How ought we to live with our Creator — as strangers or as children? How are we to worship Him—as a distant being or as near to us? What is His relation to us—that of a remote Sovereign, who takes no immediate and special care of individuals, or that of a Parent, who, whilst provident of his whole family, watches over every particular child?

These are great questions, and happily our Religion answers them fully. However indistinct Nature's teachings may be upon these points—however insufficient unassisted reason may be to establish the truth of a minute and constant Providence, extended to each single creature—however strong may be the appearances of a general order of the Universe, to which the interests of private individuals are sternly sacrificed—still as Christians we are assured, that God in His government of the whole does not forget the parts, that He is the Father of *each*, as well as of ALL intelligent beings.

It is the Perfection of Wisdom—the distinction of an All-comprehensive Mind—to embrace at once the concerns of a vast community of beings and the interest of every single member, to conjoin the enlarged views of a Universal Sovereign with the minute inspection and tender care of a Father. And such is our God. He is the God of ALL, and yet He is *my* God. At the same moment He pervades heaven and earth, taking charge of the sustenance, progress, and growing happiness of the unbounded creation, and He is present with me, as intent upon my character, actions, wants, trials, joys and hopes, as if I were the sole object of His love.

This view of God we all have a deep interest in impressing on our minds. We must strive to combine, in our conception of Him, the thoughts of a Particular and a Universal Providence. On the one hand, we must not narrow His loving care, as if it were mindful of ourselves alone, nor think of Him only as doing us good. For this would be to rob Him of his Infinitude, and darken the splendour of His boundless beneficence. Such a view would make religion the nurse of selfishness, and convert our connexion with the Supreme Being into one of self-interest. Never let us try to monopolize God. Never let us imagine that God exists only as administering to our individual wants. Never let us for an instant forget His relation to the Universe. Let us adore Him for the streams of bounty, which flow unceasingly, from the fountains of His life, to all His countless creatures. But on the other hand, beware lest in thus enlarging your views of the Infinite One, you lose your hold of the correlative truth—that though all beings of all worlds are His care, though His mind thus embraces the Universe, He is yet as mindful of you, as if that Universe were blotted out, and you alone survived to receive the plenitude of His care. God's relation to you is not an exclusive one, but it is as close as if it were. Judge not of the Infinite Mind by your own. Because you, frail men, when you extend your care over a city, a community, or a nation, overlook the concerns of Individuals through incapacity of comprehending in one view the vast and the minute, the whole and its particles, do not thence imagine, that the Infinite Spirit cannot be perpetually caring for you, because He cares for the immense Community of Spirits. Never conceive that your actions are overlooked and forgotten, because of the multiplicity of agents and beings who are to be guided and governed. Never fear that your wants are forgotten, because the boundless Creation sends up a cry to its common Father, and He has an infinite Family for whom to provide. Never think that your characters are objects of little interest, because innumerable orders of beings of higher attainments and virtues attract the regards of this munificent King. Were you His only creature alive, He could not think of you more constantly and tenderly, or be more displeased with your resistance to duty, or feel more joy in your fidelity to right, than He does now.

The human mind, apt to measure God by itself, has always found a difficulty in reconciling the two views which have just been stated. Through this propensity it fell into Polytheism, or the worship of many gods. Wanting a Deity, who would watch over their particular interests, and fearing that they would be overlooked by the Father of all, men invented inferior divinities,—gods for each particular country and nation,—and still more household gods, divinities for each particular dwelling, that they might have some Superior Power beneath which to shelter their weakness. Under Christianity even the same difficulty has been and still is felt. To this we must ascribe the exaltation of Saints into divinities in the Catholic Church. And among Protestants, not a few make the Universal Father a partial deity, and appropriate His blessings to their sect, as if fearing that they should lose a portion of His favour, by supposing Him to be as gracious to all human beings as to themselves.

I.—But there is no inconsistency in at once believing in God's Particular Providence and in His Universal Providence. He may watch over All, and yet watch over Each, as if Each were All. There is a simple truth, which may help us to

understand, that God does not intermit His attention to Individuals in consequence of his inspection of the Infinite Whole. It is this. The individual is a *living* part of this *living* whole,—vitally
connected with it,—acting upon it and reacted upon
by it,—receiving good, and communicating good in
return, in proportion to his growth and power. From
this constitution of the Universe it follows, that the
whole is preserved and perfected by the care of its
parts. The General good is bound up in the Individual good. So that to superintend the one is to
superintend the other; and the neglect of either
would be the neglect of both. What reason have I
for considering myself as overlooked, because God
has such an immense family to provide for? I belong
to this family. I am bound to it by *vital* bonds. I am
always exerting an influence upon it. I can hardly
perform an act that is confined in its consequences
to myself. Others are affected by what I am, and
say, and do. And these others have also their
spheres of influence. So that a single act of mine
may spread and spread in widening circles, through
a nation or humanity. Through my vice, l intensify
the taint of vice throughout the Universe. Through
my misery I make multitudes sad. On the other
hand, every development of my virtue makes me
an ampler blessing to my race. Every new truth
that I gain makes me a brighter light to Humanity.
I ought not then to imagine that God's interest in

me is diminished, because his interest is extended
to endless hosts of Spirits. On the contrary, God
must be more interested in me on this very account,
because I influence others as well as myself. I am a
living member of the great Family of All Souls; and
I cannot improve or suffer myself, without diffusing
good or evil around me through an ever-enlarging
sphere. My hearer, you are not to think of yourself as neglected, because God has an innumerable
company of children to care for. One of the
methods, by which He cares for these various
children, is to make provision for your progress.
The interests of others, as well as your own interests,
require that the Universal Father should watch
over your progress. For just so far as you are wise,
disinterested and happy, you will become a universal
blessing. Be not disheartened then by looking
round on the immense Creation, and thinking that
you are but one among millions; for these millions
have a *living* interest in each one. You as an individual cannot but spread good or evil indefinitely
around you, and through succeeding generations.

In these remarks we have seen, that from the
intimate and vital connexion between the Individual
and the Community of Spirits, God in taking care of
each person is taking care of the whole, and that
there is a perfect harmony between the General and
the Particular superintendence of God. From the same
vital connexion of beings, I derive another encourag-

ing view, leading to the same result. I learn from it that God's attention to his whole Creation, far from withdrawing his regard from Me, is the very method whereby He is advancing my especial good. I am organically connected with the great Family of the Universal Parent. Plainly then it is for my happiness, that this Family should be watched over and should prosper. Suppose the Creator to abandon all around me, that He might bless me alone, should I be a gainer by such a monopoly of God's care? My happiness is manifestly bound up with and flows from the happiness of those around; and thus the Divine kindness to others is essentially kindness to myself. This is no theory; it is the fact confirmed by all experience. Every day we receive perpetual blessings from the progress of our race. We are enlightened, refined, elevated, through the studies, discoveries and arts of countless persons, whom we have never seen and of whom we have never even heard. Daily we enjoy conveniences, pleasures, and means of health and culture, through advancements in science and art, made in the most distant regions. And in so far as we possess elevated, disinterested and holy characters, or enlarged intelligence, have not these been cherished and encouraged by the examples, writings, deeds and lives of far-spread fellow-beings, through all ages and nations? How much would each of us assuredly be advanced in happiness, wisdom, virtue, were the

community around us—were all the persons with
whom we hold intercourse—more humane and more
heavenly! Is God then neglecting us in his care of
others? How could He bless us more effectually,
than by carrying forward the great Spiritual System,
to which we belong, and of which we are living parts?
We may well believe that so close and vital are the
connexions throughout God's Universe—between
this world of ours and other worlds—that the
Human Race is benefited by the progress of all
other Orders of Beings. So that the Creator is
providing for your happiness and virtue, in the
care which he extends over the diverse systems of
worlds around, and over the higher ranks of Spirits
in the Heavens. This happiness we may, indeed
we do, lose by vice—by a spirit of self-love—hostile alike to the Creator and to his creatures. But
this will be our self-imposed doom. Such isolation
will not come from neglect on the part of our
Heavenly Father. For He designs to make us all
blessed beings together, in a blessed universe.

II.—Thus having seen how consistent is the
doctrine of God's care for the Whole with the doctrine that He watches minutely over every Individual, let me now ask you to look at this doctrine
more closely, in its practical applications. Consider what affecting ideas it involves! According to
this truth, we are, each one of us, present to the
mind of God. We are penetrated, each one of us,

instant by instant, by His all-seeing eye; we are known, every single person of us, more interiorly by Him, than we are known to ourselves. Moment by moment, the Living God sustains us; and His own Life continually flows into us through His omnipotent good-will. Moment by moment, He intends and does us good; and no blessing comes to us without His immediate loving purpose. In fine, and above all, the Holy One never loses sight of our character and conduct. He is present to inspire sentiments, suggestions, motives, and to grant us aids and opportunities for spiritual growth. He witnesses and delights in our virtues. And He too witnesses and condemns every sin. Let us never be unmindful of this last view. Because God is always near, intending and doing us good, we must not imagine that His relation to us will secure our happiness, if we are unworthy in spirit and in life. It is true, that nothing but good can come from God. But never let us forget that this very good may be turned into evil, through our perverseness. Let us remember—it is a solemn truth—that from our very nature our happiness is entrusted to our own keeping. We are endowed with that awful power of Free-Will, without which virtue cannot be. For ourselves we must determine, whether God's gifts shall fulfil their end in promoting happiness, or whether they shall be turned into bitterness and woe. There is not one blessing in existence, not even God's choicest gift, which may not through our neglect, abuse and perversity, become a source of misery. So that God's connexion with us, intimate as it is, is yet no pledge of happiness, without our own concurrence.

Intimate and tender, beyond our highest conception, is our Heavenly Father's relationship to us! He is incessantly our creator and renewer, our upholder and benefactor, our witness and judge. The connexion of all other beings with us, when compared with this, is foreign and remote. The nearest friend, the most loving parent is but a stranger to us, when contrasted with God. No words can adequately express this *living* alliance of the Creator with His creatures. Our bodies are less closely united with our minds, than is God with our inmost self. For the body may be severed from the soul without working its destruction. But were God to forsake this thinking principle, it would instantly perish. How near to me is my Creator! I am not merely surrounded by His influence, as by this air which I breathe. I am pervaded by His agency. He quickens my whole being. Through Him am I this instant thinking, feeling and speaking. And knowing thus the intensity and the extent of this relationship, how is it possible that I can forget Him!

My hearers, I have thus turned your attention to this sublimely affecting subject of our vital connexion with God, not for the purpose of awakening temporary fervour, but that we may feel the urgent duty of cherishing these convictions. If this truth becomes a reality to us, we shall be conscious of having received a NEW PRINCIPLE OF LIFE. The man, who has begun to understand, believe and feel, that *He*, as a Person, is an object of perpetual regard to the Infinite Creator, and that the Supreme Being takes a personal interest, not merely in his present welfare, but in his everlasting progress, has attained to vastly higher regions of thought and emotion, than one who is aware only of his connexion with the outward, mutable world, can even conceive of. Were a person, who had lived in ignorance of all beyond mere sensitive existence, suddenly to receive a clear impression of God's all-embracing Presence, he would undergo a greater change of condition, than if he were to awake some morning in a wholly new world, peopled by new beings, clothed in new beauty, and governed by laws such as he had never known by experience. He would be uplifted with the assurance, that at length he had found for his soul an All-sufficing Object of veneration, gratitude, trust and love, an unfailing source of strength for every mortal weakness, an exhaustless refreshment of his highest hope, an ever-springing fount of holy emotion, virtuous energy and heavenly joy, infinitely transcending all modes of good, to which he had been wont to look. In a word, he would be utterly transformed.

On the other hand, in degree as by faithlessness I lose sight of my intimate relationship with God, I am bereft of inward peace, of the desire for progress, of power to escape from myself. The future grows dim, and hope dies. A change comes over me like that which befals the traveller, when clouds overspread the sky, when gathering mists obscure his path, and gloom settles down upon his uncertain way, till he is lost. The light of life is a constant consciousness of Divine Fellowship. But we should not expect a sudden manifestation of the Infinite One to our souls. Gradually we must attain to this serene trust in God's all-protecting care, incessant mercy, and inspiring influence. The blessing will not be less real, because it comes upon us gently, according to our spiritual progress. There is no rest for our souls except in this ever-growing communion with the All-Perfect One.

III.—How then can we attain to an abiding consciousness of living relationship with the Living God? How can we reach the constant feeling that He is always with us, offering every aid consistent with our freedom, guiding us on to heavenly happiness, welcoming us into the immediate knowledge of his Perfection, into a loving fellowship with Himself? Some one may say: "I am conscious of having thus far lived very much as if there were no God. My mind is dull, my heart is cold. How shall I awake to perceive, to feel, to love, to serve, to enjoy this Living God of whom you speak?" There is time for but a brief reply; and

I shall confine myself to what seems to be essential, as the *first* step, in this approach to true Communion with the Father of Spirits.

My belief is, that one chief means of acquiring a vivid sense of God's Presence is to resist, instantly and resolutely, whatever we feel to be evil in our hearts and lives, and at once to begin in earnest to obey the Divine Will as it speaks in conscience. You say that you desire a new and nearer knowledge of your Creator. Let this thirst for a higher consciousness of the Infinite Being lead you to oppose whatever you feel to be at war with God's Purity, God's Truth, and God's Righteousness. Just in proportion as you gain a victory over the evil of which you have become aware in yourself, will your spiritual eye be purged for a brighter perception of the Holy One. And this in its turn will strengthen you for a yet more strenuous resistance of sin,—which will prepare you for still more intimate acquaintance with the Divine Nature and Character. This attainment to a knowledge of God and this instant resistance of Sin are most intimately and vitally related. Neither can advance beyond the other. For God, as the All-Good, can be known only through our own growing goodness. No man living in deliberate violation of his duty, in wilful disobedience to God's commands as taught by conscience, can possibly make progress in acquaintance with the Supreme Being. Vain are all acts of worship in church

or in secret, vain are religious reading and conversation, without this instant fidelity. Unless you are
willing to withstand the desire which the inward
monitor, enlightened as it always is by the Divine
Spirit, condemns, you must, you will, remain a
stranger to your Heavenly Father. Evil passions
and sensual impulses darken the intellect and sear
the heart. Especially important is it—indispensable
indeed—that self-indulgence and self-will shall be de-
terminedly withstood. While these enthrall us, never
can we comprehend the true glory of God. For His
glory is Perfect Love. If we would have our souls
become the temples of the Supreme Being, filled
with His light and joy and peace, we must utterly
cast out the foul spirits which are at enmity with
the Divine purity and disinterestedness.

Would you really know your Creator, would you
become truly penetrated with the consciousness of
His Presence, would you become indeed alive to His
Goodness, then show your sincerity by beginning at
once an unflagging warfare with that habit, that
passion, that affection, be it what it may, which conscience this moment assures you is hostile to God's
Will. You need not go far to learn how you may
gain more vivid views of God. The sin that now
rises to memory as your *bosom sin*, let this first of all
be withstood and mastered. Oppose it instantly by
a detestation of it, by a firm will to conquer it, by
reflection, by reason, and by prayer. Such a spiritual

conflict, trifling though it may appear, will do more, than can all other influences combined, to fit you for a near, strong, affectionate intimacy with your God. And without such a struggle of your will—which is but another name for Repentance—you can never draw a step nearer to the All-Holy and All-True. He will always be to you a God afar off, wrapt in clouds of terror. It is customary to recommend reading the Bible, religious worship, meditation, as means of awakening religious sensibility, and they are all important as means. I would on no account disparage them. Use them all. But use them in connexion with this primary obedience to conscience, this resolute resistance of your peculiar temptations. For without this all other means of religious discipline will but mock you. They may generate a temporary fervour, and kindle an occasional flash of devout feeling. But such religious emotion will be but local and transient, sinking into gloom when you most need its guiding light, never brightening to full day, nor filling the firmament of your soul with noontide peace.

My friends, in this discourse I have spoken to you of the great Truth, that the Infinite God is for ever around and within each one of you; that our Heavenly Father is interested *personally* in each one of you; that the Author of the Universe is as near to you as your very life; that the Giver of all good is incessantly doing you good. By comprehending this

7

Truth you can gain the means of a happiness, such as the whole world cannot give, and which no change in existence can take away. Incorporate it with your character. Let it call forth your love and trust in their intensest energy. And you will have found a resource, refuge, treasure, a fount of strength, courage, hope and joy truly inexhaustible. Earnestly strive then to open your inmost souls to the influence of the Infinite Being, till you are filled with his fulness. Are there none here, in whom this touching truth of an Everlasting Father always and instantly sustaining and quickening, recreating and renewing us, lies dormant; to whom reason, conscience, nature, tradition, the words of Jesus, the calls of countless blessings, speak ineffectually to rouse their gratitude to the Almighty Friend, from whom all blessedness flows forth? One day such hardness of heart towards the "Father of lights, from whom cometh down every good and perfect gift," will appear to us, what it really is, as the heaviest guilt that a free and intelligent creature can contract. As you love your immortal souls, withstand its fatal sway. The doom it brings is spiritual death. Seek aid from Heaven instantly and for ever to subdue it. Let the Living God be supreme in your thoughts and hearts, as He is supreme in the universe. Consecrate to Him unreservedly the Spirits which He called into being, that He might make them perfectly one with Himself.

V.

TRUST IN THE LIVING GOD.

TRUST IN THE LIVING GOD.

We trust in the Living God.—1 TIMOTHY iv. 10.

RELIGIOUS TRUST is the subject of the present discourse. I shall consider first its Principle, and secondly the Good which it is authorized to propose as an End. And my aim will be to quicken this germ of Divine Life in every soul.

Trust—Confidence—is an essential element of human nature. We begin life in a spirit of trust, and cling with confidence to our parents and the guardians of our infancy. As we advance in years, though deceived and betrayed, we still must anchor our trust somewhere. We cannot live without some being to lean on as a friend. Universal distrust would turn social existence into torture. The most miserable man in the community is he, who finds none to confide in, who believes in no kindness around him, who detects nothing but selfish indifference, or hate, at home and abroad. This universal distrust is so unnatural, indeed, that it never prevails in a sound mind. It is the first stage of insanity, and if indulged ends in overturning the reason.

We were born for confidence in other beings; and woe to him that cannot trust! Still confidence brings with it suffering; for all are imperfect and too many are false. There are none who do not sometimes disappoint us. How rare on earth is that constant fidelity, over which time and place exert no power. Almost every one is too intent on self and selfish interests, to be perfectly just or generous to those even, who lean upon him most. When purest in purpose, our best friends, through want of judgment, heart and will, confer but little of the good we long for. Trust never can find full repose, till it has found the Perfect Being, and expands under His unchanging Faithfulness into the sure hope of unbounded good.

Observe what a harmony there is between our nature and God. The principle of Trust, as we have seen, enters into the very essence of the human soul. We live by it. And yet, confined to the society of fellow-beings, our confidence is continually mocked, and sometimes yields to heart-withering scepticism as to all human good-will. Trust seeks Perfect Goodness. Its natural tendency is toward an Infinite and Immutable Being. In Him alone can it find rest. Our nature was made for God, as truly as the eye was made for the light of God's glorious image, the sun.

There are two questions to which I particularly ask your attention ·

First, what is the Principle of Religious Trust?

Secondly, what is the Good, for which we may trust in God?

I.—In answering the first of these questions, I would observe, that Religious Confidence rests on God's *Parental* Interest in INDIVIDUAL PERSONS. To apprehend and believe this truth, is to plant the germ of Trust in God. This truth is not easily brought home to the heart, as a reality. Let me try to illustrate it. When we look round upon the Creation, what strikes us first is the Law of Succession among all orders of living .beings. Plants and animals spring from others of their own kind; and, having unfolded their distinctive powers to a certain limit, pass away. The various Races continue, but the Individuals of each race come and go, appear a little while, and then vanish to make room for their successors. Man is subjected to the same law. He is born, passes through graduated stages, grows to a certain limit of maturity, and then apparently declines and disappears. The first impression given to a superficial observer of the world is, that the Individual is of no great worth in the sight of the Creator. The Race of man is upheld, and seems to be destined to perpetual existence. But the Individuals, of whom it is composed, appear to have nothing enduring in their nature. They pass over the earth like shadows cast by a flying cloud, leaving for the most part as slight a trace behind. They

break like meteors from the abyss, and are then
swallowed up in darkness. There are indeed plain
marks of kindness, in the laws of nature, under which
they for a time exist. Many provisions are made for
their enjoyment during their brief career. But the
benevolence, that gives them existence, seems more
intent on producing an endless Series of beings, each
receiving but limited and imperfect good, than on
raising the Individual to a substantial and enduring
felicity. According to this view, God is the Author
of fugitive, mutable existences, from love of variety,
multiplicity and development, however transitory
these several existences may be. If we rest in such
views of God, our Confidence must be faint. We may
indeed hope, from His power and goodness, that the
Human Race will continue, and still more that this
Race will improve. But that God will take an
enduring interest in Individuals, that Single Beings,
out of this ever-changing multitude, will attain to
exalted and imperishable good, we cannot trust.
We cannot be confident that this or that Individual
will on the whole enjoy its fair share of good; for,
whilst Nature is fruitful of provisions for the Human
Race, yet multitudes of our fellow-beings are so far
excluded from them as apparently to suffer far more
than they enjoy.

There are too many who stop at the superficial
view of Divine Providence which has now been
stated. And consequently they have no Trust in

God that deserves the name. They acknowledge Him indeed as the Author of the short-lived multitudes around them, and of the transitory good that they enjoy. But His Paternal interest in Persons they do not comprehend. They judge of God from what they see; and that is only mutable and transient. The Race of man may seem indeed to them to be perpetual; but they see no promise of perpetuity for Individuals. Accordingly they have little or no confidence in God, for themselves or for others, regarded as Persons. But every individual mind is *essentially* greater than it shows itself to be. No mind brings itself fully out in expression or action. On the contrary, what it says and does is but giving a sign of its inward power. When a man of genius produces some beautiful work of art or thought, or when a hero or philanthropist devotes himself to some grand enterprise, do you feel as if each particular effect were a measure of his spiritual energy? Does not one brilliant thought of a philosopher or poet reveal to you a Centre of intelligence, a living force of Will, which, far from being exhausted, must for ever radiate in new and brighter forms? Mind is not a power to be measured like material forces. Under new excitements every mind puts forth new faculties, not only undreamed of by others, but unknown to itself.

Now if this is true of each human mind, how can we believe that it is less true of the Divine Mind? Who,

that beholds this immense Universe, can imagine that
the Intelligence, which gave it birth, is spent, and
that nothing is to be looked for from it, but effects
precisely similar to those which we now see ? Survey
the multiplied forms of·life upon this earth, then lift
your eyes to the heavens ; and can you conceive that
He, who framed and moves these countless worlds
through boundless space, in beneficent order, has no
purposes beyond those which are unfolded to *us*,
creatures of a day ? Are we not surrounded by signs
of an Infinite Mind, and may we not be sure that
such a Mind ·must have unfathomable counsels, and
must intend to bestow unimagined good ? Can we
believe that Human Nature was framed by such a
Being for no higher spiritual development than
we now witness on this planet ? Is there not, in the
very incompleteness and mysteriousness of Man's
present existence, a proof that we do not as yet
behold the End for which he is destined; that the
Infinite Father has revealed but a minute portion of
His Scheme of boundless mercy; that we may trust
for infinitely richer manifestations than we have
experienced of His exhaustless grace ?

I have given one answer to the objection, that our
Trust in God must be measured by what we now
observe in the experience of mankind. I have said
that, from the very nature of Mind, and especially of
an Infinite Mind, we ought to expect immeasurably
greater good than we actually behold. But there is

another reply to the sceptic, and to this I invite
your particular attention. Our Trust, you say, must
be measured by what we see. Be it so. But take
heed to *see truly*, and to *understand* what you do
see. How rare is such exact and comprehensive
perception. And yet without it, what presumption
it is for us to undertake to judge the purposes of an
Infinite and Ever-living God. Whatever creature
we regard has actually infinite connexions with the
Universe. It represents the everlasting past of
which it is the effect. It bears signs of the endless
future, towards which it tends and leads the way.
He then, who does not discern in the present the
Past and the Future, who does not detect behind the
seen the Unseen, does not rightly understand it, and
cannot pass judgment upon it. The surface of things,
upon which your eye may fall, covers an Infinite
Abyss. You understand this surface, only so far as
you trace in it the signs of a mysterious Depth beneath. You say : " The Individuals of the human
race are frail, fugitive beings, springing up, growing,
passing away like the plant or brute ; and how can
we regard the Eternal God as deeply interested in
such transitory creatures, or trust in Him as pledged
to bestow on them an Everlasting Good ? " Are you
sure then that you comprehend the human being,
when you speak of him as subjected to the same law
of change and dissolution, which all other earthly
existences obey ? Is there nothing profounder in his

nature than that which you catch sight of by a casual glance? Is there no quality that takes him out of the rank of the living creatures beneath him in the scale? Are there within him no elements which betoken a Permanent and Enduring Existence?

Consider one fact only. Among all outward changes, is not every man conscious of his own Identity, of his continuing to be the same, single, Individual Person? Amidst the composition and decomposition of all substances around him, does he not feel that the thinking, feeling, willing Principle within remains One, undivided and indivisible Essence? Is there not a Unity in the Soul, that distinguishes it from the dissoluble compounds of material nature? And further, is this Person made up of mutable and transitory elements? Is it a mere reflexion and image of the passing shows of earth and sky? Is it a mere echo to the sounds which vibrate and die away in àn ever-moving creation? On the contrary, who does not know that he has faculties to seize upon Everlasting Truth, and affections which aspire to reach an Everlasting Good? Have we not all of us the Idea of Right, of a Divine Law older than time, and which can never be repealed? Is there not a Voice within the conscience, that we feel to be not a passing sound, but the delegate of the Eternal and Almighty? Have we not conceptions of Immensity, within which all finite beings are embraced,

of Absolute Being, over which no change has power?
Have we not the Idea of One, who is the same to-day,
yesterday, and for ever? Have we not capacities
for attaching ourselves to this Infinite and Immutable Being, of adoring the All-Perfect, of loving
the ineffably Good? Are we not all conscious of a
Power above all powers of nature, of choosing and
holding to this Good through life and death, though
all that is mightiest and most terrible in creation
should conspire to sever us from it?

Has such a being as man then no signs in his
nature of Permanent Existence? Is he to be commingled with the fugitive forms of the material
world? There is a wonderful passion, if I may
so speak, in human nature for the Immutable and
Unchangeable, that gives no slight indication of its
own Immortality. Surrounded with constantly varying forms, the mind is always labouring to find,
behind these transitory types, a fixed Reality, upon
which it can rely. Amidst the incessant changes of
Nature, it longs to discover some settled Law, to
which all movements are subject, and which can
never change. Indeed, the great work of science is
amidst mutation to find this immutable, universal,
and invariable Law. And what deep joy fills the
mind of the philosopher, when, throughout apparently
inextricable confusion, he can trace some great
Principle, that governs all events, and that they
all show forth! Man loves the Universal, the Un-

changeable, the Unitary. He meets bounds on every side ; but these provoke, as it were, an inward energy, by which he scales and overleaps them. His physical frame fills but a few feet of space ; and yet in thought he reaches forth to grasp and measure Immensity. He lives in moments, in mere wavelets of time ; and yet he looks backwards and forwards into Eternity. Thus the very narrowness of his existence excites in him a thought of boundless and endless life. Can you cast a hasty glance, even, on such a being as this, and say that you see nothing but evidences of a transient career ; that the Race may last, but that the Individual will be lost ; that the fleeting genera-tions of men find their best type in the vapours, which, exhaling from the ocean, gather into clouds for a moment, and then evaporate or fall in drops to the depth whence first they sprang ? You argue, you say, from what you see. But you look on men, as the savage looks on some exquisite invention, of which scarcely one of its many uses dawns upon his mind, or as the child gazes upon some beautiful work of art. Seeing, you *see* not. What is most worth seeing in man, is hidden from your view. You know nothing of Man truly, till you discern in him traces of an Immutable and Immortal Nature, till you recognize somewhat allied to God in his Reason, Conscience, Love and Will. Talk not of your know-ledge of men, picked up from the transient aspects of social life ! With all your boasted knowledge of human nature, you have but skimmed its surface. Human Nature, in its distinctive principles, is to you as yet an unrevealed mystery.

It is not then to be inferred, from what we see, that God does not take an interest in the Individual, and that He may not be trusted as designing great good for each particular Person. In every human mind He sees powers kindred to His own—the elements of angelic glory and happiness. These bind the Heavenly Father's love indissolubly to every Single Soul. And these divine elements authorize a Trust utterly unlike that which springs from superficial views of man's transitory existence.

II.—Thus are we led to the second question that I proposed to consider : What is the Good for which, as Individual Persons, we may trust in God? One reply immediately offers itself. We may not, must not trust in Him for whatever good we may arbitrarily choose. Experience gives us no warrant to plan such a future for ourselves, as mere natural affections and passions may crave, and to confide in God's Parental Love as pledged to indulge such desires. Human life is made up of blighted hopes and disappointed efforts, caused by such delusive confidence. We cannot look to God even for escape from severest suffering. The laws of the Universe, though in general so beneficent in their operation, still bring fearful evil to the Individual. For what then may we trust in God? I reply, that we may

trust unhesitatingly, and without a moment's wavering, that God desires the Perfection of our Nature,
and that He will always afford such ways and means
to this great End, as to his Omniscience seem most
in harmony with man's moral freedom. There is
but one True Good for a spiritual being, and this is
found in its Perfection. Men are slow to see this
truth; and yet it is the key to God's Providence,
and to the mysteries of life. Look through the
various ranks of existence, which fall beneath our
observation, and is not the good of every creature
determined by its peculiar Nature; and does not the
well-being of each consist in its growth towards its
own special Type of perfection? Now how can
man be happy but according to the same law of
growth in all his characteristic powers? Thus the
enjoyment of the body is found to be dependent on
and involved with the free, healthy and harmonious
development—that is the Perfection—of its organization. Impair, or derange any organ, and existence becomes agony. Much more does the happiness
of the Soul depend upon the free, healthy and harmonious unfolding of all its faculties. Intellectual,
Moral, Spiritual Perfection—or, in other words, that
life and energy of Reason, of Conscience and of
Will, which brings our whole spiritual nature into
harmony with itself, with our fellow-beings, and with
God—this alone deserves the name of GOOD. So
teaches Christianity. For this religion has for its

great end to redeem the soul from every disease, excess, infirmity and sin, to re-establish order among its complex powers, to unfold within it the principle of duty as its guiding law, and to develope it in the beauty of perfect rectitude and universal love. Now for this Good, we may trust in God, with utter confidence. We may be assured that He is ready, willing, and anxious to confer it upon us; that He is always inviting and leading us towards it by His Providence, and by His Spirit, through all trials and vicissitudes, through all triumphs and blessings; and that unless our own will is utterly perverse, no power in the universe can deprive us of it.

Such I say is the Good for which we may confide in God, the only Good for which we are authorized to trust in Him. The PERFECTION of our Nature—God promises nothing else or less. We cannot confide in Him for prosperity, do what we will for success; for often He disappoints the most strenuous labours, and suddenly prostrates the proudest power. We cannot confide in Him for health, friends, honour, outward repose. Not a single worldly blessing is pledged to us. And this is well. God's outward gifts—mere shadows as they are of Happiness—soon pass away; and their transitoriness reveals, by contrast, the only True Good. Reason and conscience, if we will but hear their voice, assure us that all outward elevation, separate from inward nobleness, is a vain show; that the most prosperous career, without growing health of soul, is but a prolonged disease, a fitful fever of desire and passion, and rather death than life ; that there is no stability of power, no steadfast peace, but in immovable principles of right; that there is no true royalty but in the rule of our own spirits ; no real freedom but in unbounded disinterested love ; and no fulness of joy but in being alive to that Infinite Presence, Majesty, Goodness, in which we live and move.

This Good of Perfection, if we will seek it, is as SURE as God's own Being. Here I fix my Confidence. When I look round me, I see nothing to trust in. On all sides are the surges of a restless ocean, and everywhere the traces of decay. But amidst this world of fugitive existences, abides One Immortal Nature. It is the Human Soul—your soul—my soul—the soul of every human being. Entirely I trust that this is Immortal, because allied by god-like powers to the Father. This Soul He created, as I believe, to become a glorious Image of Himself— to contend with and overcome all evil, to seek and receive evermore all good, to obey the eternal Law of Right, to which God's own Will conforms. In God I trust for this Infinite Good. I know no other Good for which to trust Him. Take away *this*, and I have nothing, you have nothing, worth living for. Henceforth our existence is without an End ; and the Universe itself seems to be but a waste of power.

Let not the sceptic point me to the present low

development of Human Nature, and ask me what promise I see there of that higher condition of the Soul, for which I trust. Even were there no sufficient answer to this question, I should still trust. I must still believe that surely as there is a Perfect God, Perfection must be His End; and that, sooner or later, it must be impressed upon His highest work, the Spirit of Man. Then I must believe, that where He has given truly Divine Powers, He must have given them for development. I cannot believe that He has imparted conscience, only to be trampled upon by the appetites; that He has kindled reason and the desire for goodness, only to perish in dark despair. But we are not left without another answer to objections drawn from the present low condition of the human race. Amidst its degradation are there none who show the high End of God in human nature? Are there none in whom the spirit has conquered the flesh, in whom the divine principle of love has conquered self; none to whom the voice of duty is the clearest, most persuasive, and most commanding of all sounds; none to whom God is a glorious Reality, and who are strong, calm, and serenely bright in His deeply felt Presence? Are there none who love, as Jesus loved, and who can suffer and die for their race as did the Beloved Son? There are such men. These are they, who reveal to us the true End of our Nature, the Good to which we, one and all, are destined.

Human nature is indeed at present in a very imperfect stage of its development. But I do not therefore distrust that Perfection is its End. For an end, from its very nature, is something to be attained through inferior degrees. We cannot begin with the end. We cannot argue that a being is not destined for a good, because he does not instantly reach it. We begin as children, and yet are created for maturity. So we begin life imperfect in our intellectual and moral powers, and yet are destined to wisdom and virtue. The Philosopher, whose discoveries now dazzle us, could not once discern between his right hand and his left. And the energies of an adoring Seraph were once probably wrapped up in a germ, as humble as the mind of a human infant. We are to read God's End in our inherent tendencies, not in our first attainments. With godlike capacities, it matters little what rank we hold at outset, if only the spirit be awakened in us to fulfil its destiny. To him who has entered an interminable path, with impulses which are carrying him onward to Perfection, of what importance is it where he first plants his step? The Future is all his own.

But you will point me to those, who seem to be wanting in this spirit of Progress, this impulse towards Perfection, and who are sunk in sloth or guilt. And you will ask whether God's purposes towards these are yet loving. I answer: Yes! They fail

through no want of the kind designs of God.
From the very nature of Goodness, it cannot be
forced upon any creature by the Creator; nor can
it be passively received. The Individual Person
must seek and strive for it himself, and must blame
himself only, if it be not sought and found. Each
of us should feel that our Creator is welcoming us to
our Supreme Good, and is offering strength for its
attainment. In every duty that God enjoins He
marks out the way to Perfection; in every rebuke
of conscience He warns us to turn from the way
of death. By change, disappointment, affliction,
bereavement, He seeks to win us from what is
fugitive to the one, true, Eternal End. The most
fallen human being is summoned by an inward
voice to repent; and he should trust in God, that
if he will listen to this voice, he shall be restored,
strengthened, comforted, cheered with hope from
the merciful Father, and raised from his degradation
to an angel's glory.

What a sublime doctrine it is, that Goodness
cherished now is Eternal Life already entered on!
What can be more cheering and ennobling, than the
Trust that God appoints all changes as the means of
a spiritual growth which is never to cease; that He
ordains our daily social relations, to nurture in us
a love which at length is to embrace the Spiritual
World; that He ordains trial, to awaken the power
of good-will, to which all obstacles are to yield, and

which in the progress of our being is to accomplish
miracles of beneficence, unimaginable here! What
a happiness it is, to feel assured that our education
is going on perpetually under a Father, who is making all nature, all events of providence, all society,
teachers and inspirers of truth and rectitude! What
a blessedness it is, to trust that we are to live for
ever in this Boundless Universe of an Infinite God;
that its deep mysteries are to be more and more
revealed; that more beautiful and wonderful creations are everlastingly to open before us; that we
are through ages on ages to form closer and purer
friendships throughout the vast Family of Souls,
and to diffuse our sympathies through ever-widening
spheres; that we are to approach God for ever by a
brighter vision, an intenser love, a freer communion,
and a larger participation of His Spirit and His Life!
These assurances of Trust are no dreams. They are
sublime truths, manifested in our Nature, written in
God's Word, shining out in the character of the
Beloved Son. No! They are not dreams. To each
and all of us they may become glorious Realities.
This is not a Confidence to be cherished by a select
few. Each and all of us are invited to cherish such
a Trust, and authorized by Our Father to regard
this unutterable good as the End of our being!

Thus have I spoken of religious Trust, in its Principle and its End. I have time to suggest but one
motive for holding fast this Confidence as a fountain

of spiritual strength.　We talk of our weakness.
We lack energy, we say, to be in life what in hope
we desire.　But this very weakness comes from
want of Trust.　What invigorates you to seek other
forms of good?　You believe them to be really
within your reach.　What is the soul of all great
enterprises?　It is the confidence that they may be
achieved.　It was a maxim of heathen wisdom, that
all things are possible to him who feels them to be
so.　To confide in a high power is to partake of that
power.　It has often been observed, that the strength
of an army is more than doubled by confidence in
its chief.　Confide, only CONFIDE, and you will be
strong.　You cannot conceive the mighty energy
treasured up in living Trust.　Put your Trust in
your own Spiritual Being; put your Trust in the
Living God.

My friends, do we thus trust in God?　Have
we more than mere traditional acquiescence in the
doctrine of the Divine Goodness?　Do we rely on
Him as really the Father of our Individual Spirits,
as earnestly desiring our personal progress in an
endless life?　Do we vividly feel that He is near us
as our everlasting Friend, to guide, cheer and bless
our aspirations and our efforts?　And in this Confidence do we watch, pray, strive, press forward and
seek resolutely for ourselves and fellow-beings the
highest end of existence, even the Perfection of our
Immortal Souls?

VI.

LIFE A DIVINE GIFT.

LIFE A DIVINE GIFT.

Now we have received, not the spirit of the world, but the spirit which is of God; that we might know the things that are freely given to us of God.—1 CORINTHIANS ii. 12.

No truth is more fitted to touch our hearts than the doctrine of our entire Dependence upon God as the Giver of Life. It sets before us a Goodness, from which countless blessings incessantly proceed, and a Power that can instantly withhold them. It implies the most tender and intimate relationship between ourselves and the Greatest of Beings. It impresses on every good of existence the character of a Gift. It awakens us to habitual thankfulness. It rebukes the hard heart, that lives unmindful of the all-sustaining Father. It utters remonstrance and warning against contempt of His gracious laws. It teaches that all other beings are as nothing to us, compared with this Infinite One, "who is above all and through all and in all." And it summons us to cherish a devoted love for our Divine Benefactor, more ardent, and more constant, than to any other friend.

This conviction of our Dependence, though so im-

portant, does not spring up spontaneously and fix
itself without effort in the mind. God does not
intend that we shall come to Him by compulsion.
We must watch over pious impressions, and cultivate
them, or they will never become vigorous and enduring. There is, in the very constitution of the world,
an important law, that is to a degree unfavourable to
our consciousness of dependence. No doubt, among
other purposes, it was intended to be a part of our
discipline—a trial to call forth our vigilance. The
law is this:—God has so formed us, that most of the
Goods of life require on our part exertion to secure
their attainment. Generally the rude material is
given, and the means of fashioning it to our use;
but without our co-agency, our enjoyment of nature is
unspeakably lessened. The purpose of this arrangement is obvious. It has a tendency to call forth our
faculties. Such a world is an admirable school for
intellectual and active beings. Our powers of invention, our resolution, perseverance, courage, enterprise, patience, energy, are taxed to the utmost and
grow by exertion. And thereby we receive a gratification far nobler than any passive pleasure can be—
that of hope blended with fruition. Most wise is
this method of Providence. Let us be grateful for
it. But exertion, and especially prosperous exertion,
begets the consciousness of Power, and too often the
notion of Independent Power. Surrounded by a
visible creation, on which we act with success, we

call ourselves its lords, and forget its Creator and Upholder. Our own will seems to work out our welfare. And selfishness magnifies our agency, till self-idolatry creeps in to poison all life's blessings.

There is one plain thought well suited to repress this pernicious working of pride. True, we do owe our enjoyments in a sense to our own efforts,—that is, without exertion we should not gain them. But after all, how small a proportion of the work of promoting our happiness do we perform. How little of the good can we trace to our hands. We sow the seed, which another Power has created, into that earth, which another Power has spread around us. We add a little culture, and here we stop. But how much must intervene between this exertion and gathering the ripened fruit! How many suns must rise and set, how many dews and rains distil! And what part in all these processes is due to our puny selves? Can our voice reach the clouds, and command one drop to fall on the parched earth? Is it through our direction, that the root projects its tendrils through the soil—that the light stalk springs up—and the flower unfolds its beauty to the sun and sheds its fragrance through the air? In like manner we hew from the forests, which were growing ere our birth, materials for our ships, and exult in our prosperous voyages. But does the sea with its tides and currents flow by our control? Are the winds our ministers? And do the products of other

climes grow through our influence? Thus the present system is beautifully contrived to give a field for
exertion, and yet to inculcate the lesson of dependence. Our blessings come through our own labour;
but they have connexions so immense, and are influ-
enced by causes so entirely removed from our guidance, that our dependence is taught in the very
moment of overflowing triumph. This lesson is
taught, however, only to those who are disposed to
learn. God forces wisdom upon none. We may live,
not recognizing His Power, and idolizing our own;
and thus turn our very effort into crime, and our
blessings to a curse.

My friends, how can I aid you in deepening this
sense of Dependence? Let me enumerate a few of
our best known blessings, to show the witness which
they bear to a Higher Power than our own, for ever
sustaining us

I.—HEALTH is a priceless blessing. It is often
called the greatest of blessings; and we are told, that
without it life has no worth. This language is too
strong. It has been my happiness to know those
who, amidst infirmity and frequent illness, through
force of intellect, and still more through religious
principle, devout gratitude and trust, have found life
a greater boon than the multitude of the strong and
healthy ever dream of. Still, Health is an inestimable
good, and is essential to the full development and
gratification of our powers. When possessed with-

out interruption, however, it is peculiarly apt to beget thoughtless presumption and proud self-confidence. Yet one may justly wonder how the healthiest even can for a moment forget the Giver of Life; for hardly a blessing can be named so little under our control as health. True, temperance and observance of sanitary laws undoubtedly may protract existence, if we consider human society on a large scale. But the individual has in his temperance no pledge of safety. Health is the harmony, balance, and well-proportioned action of innumerable organs, fibres, nerves, muscles, blood-vessels, membranes, of which most men know comparatively nothing. And a casual derangement in some minute cell, which we cannot discern, and of which we never heard, may begin the work of destruction that will lay the strongest in his grave. A tiny nerve, so slightly wounded that the microscope cannot detect the injury, will rack the whole body with agony. Who of us can look within this complex frame, and discover the first faint flush of an inflammation, that is soon to become a hectic burning on the cheek, and a consuming fire in the lungs? Who can trace out, in some subtle vessel unconsciously ruptured, the elements of disease and dissolution? We go forth exultant, and quicken our blood by the glow that health pours through our limbs; and yet we find, in the very freshness of the air, ordinarily so invigorating, a check of some vital function, and date fatal illness from the chance breath of a north wind.

And health is not the prey of these obvious risks only. There is something inexplicable in its subtle changes. Suddenly we sicken, we know not why or how. Languor creeps over us. We feel as a burden our common labours. The relish for food, air, exercise, recreation, is blunted. Life loses its bright charm, and gradually declines by mysterious decay. Does the sight of such sudden changes stir us up to new vigilance; and do we hope, by increased care, to escape the common danger? Then this very anxiety becomes a worse peril than those we seek to shun. Timidity as to our health not only may subject us to imaginary illness, but bring on real disease. The hypochondriac, shrinking from every breeze, weighing his food, and fearing exhaustion from fatigue, loses all animation. And by flight he meets sooner the death he dreads. The continuance of health to beings so delicately and exquisitely framed, and plunged among so many sources of disease, is indeed a constant miracle. It ought to affect us deeply. A day, closed without suffering, should be to us an affecting witness of God's loving care. And we should wake each morning with something of the emotion, that a new Gift of Life would call forth. It is really God who gives us health. To His Inflowing Energy we owe the vigorous muscle, the strong arm, the firm tread.

Through His all-quickening aid do we walk abroad to find the air balmy, mere motion pleasure, occupation attractive, society cheering, and our common existence a continual joy.

My hearers, do not let health generate self-reliance. Receive it, and use it gratefully as God's Gift. Young man, abuse not and waste not in excess, that should make you blush, this Divine blessing. To you, let the elastic step, bloom on the cheek, the bright eye, the smooth brow, and delight in fresh existence, speak of God the Giver. Thank Him for health. Consecrate it as His trust to innocent enjoyment, manly effort, social usefulness, and preparation for an honourable and holy career.

II.—Our Dependence upon God, the Giver, for PROPERTY, is the next topic that suggests itself. This is so trite a theme that one has hardly courage to touch upon it. Men have heard from their birth that riches "take wings and fly away." The instability of human fortune has been the commonplace of moralists. All lands and ages have seen flourishing families reduced to want, and the once wealthy compelled to beg the aid which they before bestowed. And such vicissitudes have been set forth in popular proverbs, and by prophets and poets, as monuments of Providence, to teach men not to trust in uncertain riches, but to use them as talents lent, which are to be accounted for. Would that a truth so plain needed no enforcing ! But among ourselves wealth still feeds presumptuous pride. The rich man is described, by distinction, as " independent." And the multitude toils for wealth, as the means of " independence." That property is in no measure under human influence, or that industry, prudence, caution, can do nothing to gain and secure it—we need not affirm, for the purpose of teaching dependence. Men undeniably do something towards determining their own fortunes. But let the most prosperous man look back, and he will confess how much of his success must be ascribed to seeming accident,—that is, to unlooked-for propitious coincidences. How often do enterprises, which inspired most hope, fail; whilst others, from which little was anticipated, become the foundation of princely opulence! You have " succeeded " through life! And why ? Because you came into life at a happy season. You took the tide at its influx. And if that moment had been lost, no effort, however strenuous, could have brought back the golden opportunity. Some great public event, over which you had no control, forwarded your private plans. An earlier occurrence of a storm, the failure of others in business, a commercial revulsion, a war, might have involved you in inextricable embarrassment. Others as sanguine as yourself, whom perhaps your success emboldened, entered on the same field of enterprise, to reap only disappointment and penury.

The mode of acquiring Property which is most common in our large cities—trade—has well been called a "lottery." And although trade is made more insecure than it need be, through the spirit of rash adventure, yet, when conducted with utmost sobriety, it is still of necessity a sphere of constant hazard. The calculations, which it requires, are too extensive and complicated for the largest mind to grasp. And the laws of consumption and supply are so intricate, that the most judicious may err. Thus Property has found in all times its fittest symbol in the fluctuating ocean, upon whose breast so much of it is won. The progress of society has as yet done little to make property secure. Providence has appointed, apparently, that with wealth's increase its tenure should become more unstable, as if thus to teach more powerfully man's dependence. Formerly, there was less wealth among us, but it was more sure and steadfast. There were fewer overgrown fortunes, and smaller incomes; but property being chiefly in real estate, and invested in houses or lands, underwent fewer fluctuations. Now, by improvements in machinery, the increase of personal property, the vast development of credit, and the extension of commerce, the pecuniary connexions of men and of communities are becoming indefinitely multiplied. The complexity of business is increased. Vast operations, requiring the joint means and efforts of multitudes, are carried on with ever-augmenting speed, and competition is inflamed almost to madness. The result of this extensive intercourse, and of these widespread connexions and dependencies, is, that the property of the humblest as well as the highest is affected by political, social, industrial events in every quarter of the civilized world. A single bankruptcy may give a shock to commercial centres that is felt in every home throughout all nations. Every man is now affected by what are called "the times"—a significant word, so well expressing the changing state of the community. Commercial depressions and panics spread distress far and wide. The suspension of great establishments reduces to idleness crowds of resourceless labourers. And the largest capital of persons and communities is dispersed more rapidly even, than it was accumulated. Thus fortunes rise and fall, like billows in a storm-tossed sea. Hence the prevalent anxiety about property,—an evil that makes so serious a deduction from the comforts, gained by our improved condition in the productive arts and in commerce.

Such evils and trials surely should deepen a spirit of reliance on the overruling Providence of God. A scene of such vicissitude is certainly a school to teach dependence. In a world so inconceivably complex, success should be religiously referred to the Supreme Power. The rich man should feel that it is God who has made him to differ in his lot from his poorer brother, and apportioned alike his duties and his privileges. Wealth should be held as a *trust* from the Great Proprietor. We should remember that what we properly call our own in reference to fellow-creatures, is not *our own* in reference to our Creator; but is subjected by Him to the supreme law of immutable Right. Social laws may hedge round our possessions from human violation; but they are powerless to guard, when God wills to humble us by the resumption of His Gifts. Lightning, fire, frost, storm, blight, mildew, public calamities, political disturbances, and innumerable influences whereby God moulds the destiny of nations and of individuals, heed not the enactment of human legislators. We are as vulnerable in our Property as in our persons. The very means we use to increase it may insure its destruction. The human agents, by whom we would build it up, may waste and prostrate it.

Make not wealth then your dependence. Associate it habitually in your thoughts with God the Giver. Seek it from Him; and consecrate it to Him. Where Property is gained and enjoyed in a self-relying spirit, without a thought of the Heavenly Giver, its loss becomes an overwhelming blow. The mind, unused to lean on a Higher Power, has no support left, when material resources are gone, and has often been known to sink into despair, and

in half-insanity to cast away life itself as worthless.

III.—We depend on God for INTELLECT. In the
present age peculiar honour is rendered to mental
power; and perhaps no possession inspires more
Self-elation and Self-dependence. Mind is indeed
a noble gift; but still it is a Gift. We receive it
from the Father of Spirits. And we hold it by
an awfully uncertain tenure. Let the consciousness
of this strengthen our humble conviction of entire
dependence. That we have, in some degree, power
over our own minds, we all feel. That industry, research, study, enrich the intellect, and that thoughts
stored up in memory become to an extent our
property, we all know. Accordingly, Biography is
full of prodigies of learning, of men whose minds
were treasuries of various knowledge. These intellectual giants too often have felt as if by their
own efforts they had raised themselves above the
common herd.

But there is one consideration particularly suited
to abate this self-reliance of Genius. It is this.
However abundantly knowledge may have been
accumulated, by observation, study, or reflection,
the vividness with which these remembered thoughts
shall recur to the mind, and in which their chief
worth consists, is not within our power. A man of
talent may bring back indeed his former views; but
he cannot at pleasure recall them with that energy,

which insures their efficient influence over other
minds. He strives to speak or to write with vigour,
but gives forth tame utterance only. His mind no
longer is borne onward as by pinions, but, like
a machine, must be impelled by foreign force.
His words come no more from the soul. After his
best preparation he is spiritless. His animation is
not spontaneous, joyful, and free; but he tugs at his
load, like a weary hack, chafed by the lash into
momentary speed. Hence it is that Genius so often
disappoints itself and its admirers. Self-dependent,
self-centred, self-confident, when it would do most,
it finds itself incapable and helpless. It ought to
learn humility from the fact, that its happiest efforts
come from an unexpected and inexplicable fervour,
which it can neither command nor detain.

It is nowise my meaning, of course, to depreciate
study or intellectual toil. But study and toil as we
may, we cannot infuse into the mind, *at will*, that
living energy which is its Inspiration. Mere knowledge seems to be, in some degree, permanent and
under our control; but that inward fire and force
of intellect, on which the usefulness of knowledge
depends, is of all possessions most insecure. Wealth
is as available at one hour of the day as another, and
it may be so invested as to be insured from ordinary
changes. But the Life of Intellect—how mutable
it is ! There are hours of every day when it droops.
Sometimes weeks may pass, and no bright thoughts

will visit us. Sadly we feel that the lustre of our
intellectual day is dimmed. The light that irradiates
the mind does not shine with the steadiness of the
sun. The eclipses of that orb we can foretell. Its
rising and setting we anticipate. But the sun of the
soul rises and sets we know not how. Its radiance
fades when we most look and long for its brilliant
beams. That Sun of the intellect—what is it? May
it not be God, in a more direct sense than we imagine ?
That glowing splendour, that fervid heat, which
sometimes burst upon the soul, and give it new
rapidity and reach of thought, new warmth and
loftiness of feeling—whence come they ? Are they
not radiations from the Parent Mind ? Are they
not His immediate Gift ?

Books without number have been written on the
human mind, and many of the laws, according to
which its thoughts are associated, have been traced.
But the higher workings of the mind—its diviner
intuitions, its spiritual conceptions, its apparently
self-originated ideas—have never been explained.
They come and go, we know not whence or whither.
We may give some account of the manner in which
a particular train of thought was first suggested to
a man of Genius. But the life which he breathes
through his ideal representation, the hues which
he throws round it, the splendour in which he
arrays it, the tone of tenderness or sublimity in
which he embodies it, the more than lightning

speed by which he blends it with remote conceptions, the harmony in which he places it with
universal truth, the vital force by which he sends
it far and deep to quicken the souls of hearers
or readers, and awakes in them new worlds of
thought and feeling:—these are inexplicable mysteries. Philosophy cannot reveal their origin or modes
of action. They can only be felt by experience.
The Man of Genius himself, in putting forth these
powers, is most conscious that he cannot command
them. They come not at his bidding; they stay
not at his pleasure. If a devout man, he thanks God
for these influxes of mental illumination, as peculiar
communications of His Intellectual Energy, and
prays that he may be more and more open for the
reception of these Heavenly Gifts.

IV.—Next I propose to show that we depend on
the Divine Being for MORAL and RELIGIOUS POWER,
and that the very Spiritual Energy, whereby we grow
in personal goodness, is God's Gift. This view of
our dependence is incomparably the most important
for us constantly to cherish. And yet this conception of the intimate relationship between our own
Will and the Will of our Heavenly Father is encompassed with peculiar difficulties. Let me invite then
that serious attention, without which so profound a
truth can never be apprehended aright.

There are those who, when they hear it asserted,
that they depend on God for moral and religious life,

for rectitude and holiness, are inclined to say: "What!
have we no Power of our own to know the Right,
to feel the Good, to practise Virtue? If not, whence
springs our consciousness of obligation? Without
Power, there can be no responsibility. Deny us this,
and we cease to be subjects of a Moral Government.
We ourselves, and not another for us, must determine
our own conduct and character, or no praise or blame
can attach to us for the discharge or neglect of
duty." This objection is founded in truth, and
deserves careful consideration. Every man's heart
tells him, that until he have Power over his own
character, Power to determine his own conduct, he is
not answerable for his feelings or actions, and cannot justly be rewarded or condemned, let him
think or do what he may. God may give me other
good, such as health, without any effort of my own.
I may receive it at birth. I may retain it without
care. But Goodness cannot be thus given. Even
Omnipotence cannot *make* me a proper object of
esteem without my own activity. No act is virtuous, but such as springs from a man's own choice
and will. He cannot be good, in the moral import
of that term, any further than he determines himself towards goodness. And every man who con-
sults the inward monitor, and inquires why and
when he blames or commends himself, will find that
these judgments are founded on the consciousness
of his having this Spiritual Power. It does depend

on the individual, therefore, whether he will be good or bad.

How then, it may be asked, is man dependent on God for his virtue? Why is he to seek it from God, if the Power of securing it is lodged in his own breast? The difficulty is one which has often been felt. The apparent incompatibility of man's Moral Dependence with the Moral Freedom necessary to constitute him an accountable agent has led different sects to give up one or the other of these seemingly contradictory elements. Not a few Christians, in their anxiety to assert human Dependence, and to declare piety and virtue to be gifts of God's Grace, do in effect deny Personal Power. They teach that men are utterly weak, and speak of religion as a life infused by the irresistible agency of the Holy Spirit. The just inference from this would be, that religion has no more *moral* worth than a fair face or a large estate, or any other providential favour. And when, instead of drawing such an inference, the teachers of this doctrine proceed to threaten with the fires of everlasting torment unfortunate beings who are not visited by Almighty Grace, they utter a doctrine against which reason and conscience protest as outraging alike the Equity and the Mercy of God. There are other Christians, who, to save human accountableness, and to give man a right feeling of Power, have banished from sight his Dependence, or at least have not urged it in the strong language used in the Scriptures, and by Saints in all ages, so as to make it the foundation of solemn duties. In this way immense spiritual injury has been done. For, as I apprehend the laws of life, without a deep sense of our Dependence upon the All-Good for virtue and piety, no great improvement in either can be made.

Thus, have I stated the two classes of errors into which men have fallen, through the difficulty of reconciling Human Power with Dependence on God. How then may these two great truths be held harmoniously? How may we combine the feeling of accountableness with the conviction that we have no Goodness, and can have none, but as a Divine Gift?

There are two views which seem to me fitted to impress our constant Dependence on God for spiritual growth, without taking from us our feeling of Moral Power.

1. The first is this. Our Power over our character and conduct is the result of our Nature, of the *Constitution* of our minds. We are capable of virtue, because we are gifted with Reason, with Conscience, and with what may be called the Self-determining Principle, through which we may adopt conscience and reason as our rule. Take away these faculties, and we can do neither right nor wrong. And for want of these the inferior animals apparently are not and cannot be proper objects of praise or

blame. These high faculties are the very root of our
Moral Agency and Responsibility. Now whence
came these faculties, and how are they sustained?
Whence originated our nature, with its ineffably
grand endowments? These are God's Gifts. We
owe to Him our Spirits—this light of Reason, these
monitions of Conscience, this Power of making Conscience and Reason our guide. And we not only
received these faculties at first, but they are constantly upheld by Him who originally gave them.
Without God's Indwelling Energy, these inward
spiritual forces would expire. As the light of the
sun in the morning returns to us through God's
power,—so through the Divine Agency the light
of the mind rises anew when we awake; and without Him, we could no more bring back thought
and moral feeling, than we could restore the dawn
and the splendour of day. It is true that our
present good dispositions and purposes, if such we
have, are the results of past good acts, and in so
far we owe them to ourselves. But the Power
through which those acts were done was an organic
element of our nature, which God conferred. Still
more we owe to God that wonderful principle of
mind called "Habit," through which our present
character is vitally interwoven with the past,
through which good deeds propagate and perpetuate
themselves, and every virtuous effort makes the
next more spontaneous and successful. That I am

the purer now for former self-denial, the freer for
past obedience, is the result of that Constitution
of mind, which God originally gave, which God
continually sustains. On God, therefore, I depend
for my growth and progress.

Let me add, further, that our Nature, with all its
high moral powers, would be wholly ineffectual to
develope piety and virtue, were we not placed in a
Social Sphere, a Moral Community, in which these
powers may find scope and incitements to action.
Place a man alone, with no influences around to
speak to him of God, with no fellow-beings to be the
objects of affection, of justice and charity, with no
instruction to enlighten, no example to guide and
inspirit, and his Power would lie dormant and inert.
He would have no duties to perform, and not even
the Idea of Duty would quicken him. Our moral
and religious acquirements, so far as we have any,
are the results, not simply of our nature, but also of
our social condition—of our relations with Humanity,
of our opportunities of being acted upon by and of
acting and reacting with our Race. And Who placed
us where we are; knit us thus to others by so many
ties of love ; made us living members of the Spiritual
Universe, and opened our ears and hearts to the instruction and incitements which the laws of Divine
Order for ever utter ? We owe to God these outward means, motives, and opportunities, as truly as
we do the innate capacities of virtue and of holiness.

Without Him, then, we could do nothing. We owe to Him, as the Author of our Nature and Social State, our whole moral and religious development. Without His enlivening Agency, the Monitor within would never again speak, the intuitive perception of Duty would fade away, the Power of adhering to the Right would perish. When we wake, with a new day, how intensely should we feel, then, that it is through God's *sustaining Energy*, that the Voice of the Soul, which whispers to us with aspiration, courage, cheerful hope, again is audible, that it is the Almighty Renewer who grants us Power to make the future an improvement on the past.

This sentiment of our constant Dependence cannot be too deep. And it is plain that it in no way interferes with our exercise of Moral Power, or impairs our Moral Freedom. On the contrary, it pre-supposes that we have Power, and only teaches that this Power is a Gift. But because a gift, is it less *real*, less our *own*, or are we less *responsible* for its use? Is it not, indeed, the one unalterable sign and sanction of responsibility, that our Power is entrusted by a Higher Being, who, as the All-Good, has the *right* to demand an account of the way in which this entrusted Power is employed? Thus we learn, that as God created, and sustains our Spiritual Nature, and the Spiritual Universe, with which we are vitally related, we are bound to ascribe our moral and religious growth to His Gift, at the very time when we regard it, in an important sense, as our own work. Such is my first illustration.

2. But this does not exhaust the subject. It is plain that Scripture reveals a profounder doctrine of Dependence than this. It not only teaches that God gives sustenance to the Nature which He for ever recreates, but it affirms that He imparts INFLUENCE *additional* to this Indwelling Energy in our nature. It declares that Our Father gives His SPIRIT to them that ask. And by this we are to understand not merely that He endows us with rational and moral faculties, and the natural means of improving them, for these we enjoy whether we ask or not. But the meaning is, that He imparts an Influx of Light and Strength in answer to Prayer, and that, without this *Spiritual Aid*, we cannot grow to Perfection. According to this doctrine, our dependence for moral and religious excellence is constant and complete. But I maintain that such dependence in no way encroaches on human power, and that it still leaves the formation of our character to our own choice and will.

Am I asked how I reconcile man's Moral Power with Spiritual Influence? The answer is not difficult. Man needs and depends on the Divine Energy for his development. But this Energy he can gain, if he will *seek* for it. God liberally places it within his reach. Without it he cannot fulfil his destiny; but he is endowed with Power to aspire after it, and the Father welcomes him to its amplest use. I do not deny man's ability to acquire goodness, by saying that he must receive it from the All-Good. If by seeking he may obtain this Energy, it really becomes his own; and all the virtue it bestows is as truly under his control as if he attained it by unassisted will. Power does not consist in our being able to accomplish ends by isolated action, without using the influence of others. Man is strong, not by exercising unaided energy; but he grows in strength, in proportion as he can gather and turn to use the energies of other beings. We see an illustration of this in all common affairs. The mightiest operations of man are performed, not by his single arm, but by availing himself of the forces of nature, of wind, fire, steam, and mechanic powers. His strength multiplies itself by applying, and thus making his own, the strength of countless other agents.

The same truth is illustrated, in a higher form, in the realm of duty and religion. When I resolve on seeking spiritual improvement, do I accomplish my end by lonely efforts of my own will, however often renewed? Certainly not! I avail myself of incentives, guidance, encouragement, aid, from fellow-beings. I read what saints and sages have written, and strive to infuse their thoughts and spirit into my own soul. I recall the examples of the devout and disinterested, the heroic and humane. I associate with the excellent and wise, who live around me. I add to private intercourse and friendship the public means of religious and moral culture, worship with the congregation, communion at Christ's table, concert in deeds of charity. In a word, I strive·to grow in goodness, by absorbing and assimilating, and so making my own, the goodness and wisdom of my race. What immense help do such influences afford me! How continually, when my mind is dull and languid, do the thoughts, tones, looks of fellow-men, kindle a new flame within. How repeatedly, when my purpose faints and flags, does a cheering word, or bright example, revive my sinking energy! Facts of this kind are of such constant occurrence, that no one can dispute them. And they clearly reveal the nature of the Power which man exerts in moulding his own character. It is the Power of exalting and perfecting it, by using the inspiring aid of fellow-beings. Now Christianity teaches that in addition to all such influences, received from the life of Humanity, we need an Influence from the Father of Spirits,—which is infinitely more efficient, and without which these other aids will fail of their highest effect. It teaches also that this Divine Influence is more within our reach than the assistance derived from any or all human beings. For it is promised in full measure, in proportion as it is earnestly asked for, to all who seek. And prayer may be offered always, everywhere, and under all conditions.

That we do thus depend on the Divine Spirit, that we do thus need Heavenly Influence in the work of attaining to the Perfect Life, none who enter on this upward course can long doubt. You, who never attempted to reach this sublime end, may question or deny. To you it may seem no great task to become what you call good; for your standard of goodness is low. You never lifted your eyes to the heavenly height, to which Conscience and Christianity summon you. And in the next place, you never seriously undertook to master your passions. You are unable, as yet, to measure their might. You know not how formidable appetite, ambition, avarice are; for you have been all your life in league with these foes of your virtue. Never will you learn what sway they have usurped over you, and the strength of the chains they have bound around you, until you strive to shake them off. Then will these tyrants start up in giant form, and laugh to scorn your faint resistance, and appal your feeble will.

The good man, the true saint, the real Christian,—he who seems most spiritually self-subsistent, —will be the last to question and deny his need of Almighty Aid. He feels his dependence ever more deeply. When heavenly aspirations enter the soul, they are like a light suddenly kindled in the dark. They reveal undreamed-of defects. They waken a new sense of sin. They display the de-

formity of motives, from which we had before acted
without misgiving. The good man daily acquires
a delicacy of moral perception and feeling, before
whose penetrating gaze his inmost imperfections
are laid bare. His outward blemishes, his grosser
faults, may be amended. But the sins which cling
closest, which wind themselves subtly through the
fibres of his nature,—his pride, vanity, self-conceit,
self-indulgence, and, above all, the disloyalty of his
self-will to the Will of the All-Good,—these grow
only more apparent. He finds that to purify the
fountain-head of emotion in the soul, to cleanse its
depths from all that defiles it, to drive out lurking
ill from its recesses, and to untwine the serpent
coils of selfishness from his purposes and plans, his
aims and interests, is a vastly harder work than
building fair walls of outer decorum. Some powerful excitement, some unwonted trial, will rouse into
action lawless impulses, over whose subjection he
had sung songs of triumph. Long dormant evils,
awakened by adverse temptations, by a rush of
prosperity, or a shock of adversity, by flattery and
favour, or by persecution and peril, will burst
forth from their hiding-places, with such violence
as almost to make him doubt the reality of his religious life. At such trying seasons, a secret ejacu-
lation, a cry of the soul for God's grace to rescue,
brings home to the good man his instant dependence. With what grateful joy does he then hold

fast to the assurance, that he is never alone, for the Father is with him, that the Living Source of all good is near to him as his own life, and ready to renew him with light and strength from heaven.

I close this discourse with observing, that our Dependence upon God, the Giver, will be felt by us just in proportion as we comprehend the Spirituality of religion,—as we rise above professions and dogmas, rites and creeds, and learn that holiness and goodness consist in Love, in pure and disinterested affections and acts towards our Heavenly Father and our fellow-beings. And he who desires not only to outwardly worship, but to intimately commune with his Creator and Sustainer, he, who would gain an ever quicker sensibility to the Presence of his constant Benefactor, soon learns— that, owing to the infirmity of human powers, the illusions of the visible world, and the invisibleness of the Infinite One, it is most difficult to gain and keep the height of spiritual vision. Still, if his heart has been truly touched by a Divine Influence, he continually strives to reach this interior and enlarging knowledge of Him, "in whom we live and move and have our being." Evermore he aspires to gain—as good men have in all ages,—that unreserved, spontaneous, cheerful consecration of his highest powers, which he feels to be due to the Best of Beings. Earnestly he longs for that veneration, affectionate

devotedness, and serene trust, which may elevate
every act into adoring service of the All-Holy, for
a gratitude, beyond words to utter, that surrenders
all to Him who first bestowed,—for an escape out of
every selfish care, anxiety, fear and sorrow, into
entire, confiding, Filial Love. This near access to
the Father, this living fellowship with the Father,
becomes to him the one end of existence. But this
good, above all other goods, makes him feel only
more intensely his constant dependence on the Divine
Spirit. For this happiness of Heaven can come
only from Heaven. To the exhaustless Fountain of
Celestial Bliss he looks then with unfailing faith.
And when, in the course of his pilgrimage, this
Blessedness is granted; when calmness, which earthly
discord cannot disturb, diffuses itself through his
soul; when the clouds which hang over futurity
vanish, and the heavenly home opens before him
with ineffable splendour; when the Father's Presence
is felt like that of a visible Friend, and the parental
love of the All-Perfect penetrates his inmost being,
suffusing his eyes with tears of thankfulness, and
lifting them upward with immortal hope,—in such
high moments, whence does he consciously derive
this unutterable joy? By experience he then knows,
as well as feels, that this Peace past all understanding is the Influx of the Peace of God. With
mingled gratitude and awe, he recognizes then,
that above, upon, within his own spirit is moving

the Divine Spirit, bringing the Light of an Eternal Day. Thenceforth the truth, written in his heart by the finger of God Himself, becomes a glorious reality, that to all who ask for His Holy Spirit, the Father GIVES.

VII.

THE TRUE END OF LIFE.

THE TRUE END OF LIFE.

I must work the works of Him that sent me, while it is day.—
JOHN ix. 4.

THE END, for which a being is made, must be determined by its Nature. In proportion as we know the
powers, properties, structure of the various orders
of Creation, we are prepared to comprehend the
Good for which they are severally designed. In
regard to inferior creatures — mineral, plant, or
animal—their End is easily understood, on account
of the comparative simplicity of their constituent
elements, and because they obey unerringly their
laws of existence.

But when we come to Man, we are beset with
difficulties. Man is not simple in his organic elements. He unites in himself Two Natures, apparently quite dissimilar, the Physical and the
Spiritual. Nor is he subjected by *necessity* to the
Laws of the Universe. He has inward FREEDOM—
Freedom of Will—a power of following the Law of
his own Mind, in opposition to all outward impulse.
Accordingly, what infinite variety there is in human
pursuits! What vacillations and inconsistencies of

purpose! What vastness of desire, what extravagance of enterprise! What a contrast between the unchanging instincts of the brute and the tumultuous conflicts, hopes and fears, the lightning thoughts and boundless aspirations of the Human Soul!

I.—How then shall we determine the End of the Human Being? Why was he made—this mysterious creature,—driven by so many impulses, gifted with such diverse powers, and free to turn them in such countless directions? I have said that the End of a being is manifested in his Nature. And what does Man's Nature teach?

1. When we look upon our Race for an answer to this question, the first object that strikes our view is Man's Physical Organization, connecting him with the external world. We see in him a being with a material frame, receiving influences from the light, air, and earth, exposed to suffering from the elements, needing perpetually fresh supplies of energy from abroad, hungering and thirsting for food, shivering from cold, seeking shelter from heat, impelled by continually recurring animal wants, and under these impulses spending the largest part of existence in making provision for the body. For instance, when we pass through the streets of a City, what tides of busy life flow to and fro! What ceaseless activity drives on the rushing crowds! What hurry is in their steps! What care is stamped upon their brows! How many wheels are ceaselessly roll-

ing! What various trades are plied! What count-less warehouses are loaded with the products of all soils! How are endless fields vexed with plough-shares, and the remotest seas cleft with keels, to supply their stores! And this incessant activity has for its chief aim to gain subsistence for the body, to prolong animal life, to clothe, nourish, gratify, adorn, the animal frame. The first impression which the sight of such a City would give certainly is, that Human Nature is made for an Animal End. The houses, which densely line its streets and squares, have for their primary purpose to protect the body. The vast multitudes, which throng its thoroughfares, seem to be a collection of beings brought together to wage a defensive war against the material elements. And it must be confessed that when we enter into conversation with these bustling crowds, our first impression is confirmed. For bodily gratification does indeed appear to be the chief recompense that stimulates their thought and toil.

So much must be granted. But have we then reached the great End of human life? Because man was made to toil for subsistence and physical enjoy-ment, was he made for nothing more? In what has been thus far said have we exhausted Man's Nature? Has he no powers but such as fit him to act upon the material world? Is this his highest vocation? In reply to these questions, I shall select a few con-siderations which are very simple, and yet well suited to show that the great purpose of our being is *not* outward physical good.

2. It deserves attention then, first of all, that although Man is made to labour for the body, he manifests in this very labour a Nature vastly higher than the body. In the very act of providing for wants, which he shares in common with the animal, he shows himself to be more than an Animal. It has sometimes been said to man's reproach, that he is doomed to more servile toil than the beast of the field; that no creature is so plainly marked out for work as he; that on no other does such a burden rest. He must earn his bread in the sweat of his brow. But in this Work he puts forth faculties of which no animal manifests a trace. Thus man's very toil becomes a sign of his greatness, and indicates a higher End of life than mere bodily existence. In providing for outward good, what a profusion of Mental and Moral Power does man display! To preserve this frail physical frame, how far and wide does the human mind range in thought! What vast depths it pierces, what various materials does it combine; what active energies, what fruitfulness of resource, what profound calculation, what courage in difficulty, what invention, patience and• fortitude in unexpected danger, does it reveal! To procure subsistence, comfort and pleasure for the body, the human intellect has explored all kingdoms of nature, penetrated the mine and wrought the various metals,

traversed the sky with instruments of vision to find guidance across the seas, analyzed the constituent elements of all substances, risen to a perception of the great laws which guide the universe, gaged its mechanic forces, detected its chemical affinities, and grasped its all-embracing principle of gravitation. For the sake of preserving the body, in a word, Mind has expended an intellectual energy, boundless and expansive as the Universe itself. Can we bring ourselves to believe, then, that this Mind was made only for the body, the greater for the less, the unlimited and ever-growing Spirit for a short-lived organization of dust? Can it be that a power of Intellect, so unmeasured and exhaustless in its range, has been brought into being merely to drudge for an animal existence? How could such waste of Mind be reconciled with the wisdom of the Uncreated Mind!

There is something very convincing as to Man's true End, in the familiar facts, which have thus been unfolded. Man, when most an animal, shows himself to be more than an animal. In providing for his material nature, he reveals a higher Spiritual Nature. In living for the external world, he proves himself to be superior to that world. We need not go beyond man's physical pleasures, to feel that a nobler Spiritual Pleasure is the End of his being. Take, as a simple example, a festive entertainment, intended to fill every sense with delight. When we look at the richly-spread board, what most impresses us? Is it not this? What astonishing energies of Intellect have been lavished to provide this spectacle! What profound inquiries of science, what sagacious experiments, what trials of skill, were required to produce even the goblet from which we are to drink! What stores of artistic knowledge, what refinements of taste, what creative imagination, have conspired to work the metals into these beautiful ornaments which gratify the eye! The graceful forms of these vessels have come down to us from distant ages, and bear witness to the gathered experience and research of antiquaries and historians, as well as artists. How many of these luxuries, too, have been borne hither from the ends of the earth, across stormy oceans, through countless agencies of trade, by the triumph of human thought and will over the natural elements! This very feast, at which the self-indulgent may sink, so far as he can, into a brute, shows man to be made for Science, Philosophy, Art, Society, and gifted with powers of mental skill to which it is impossible to set bounds.

3. I have spoken of the vast amount of intellectual energy expended on the care of the body. Let me next ask you to consider the minute measure of animal good which results from this prodigious outlay of mental effort. If the fruit of our labour was immeasurable accumulation of animal pleasures, we might be tempted to think we were created for

these as an End. But are we not greatly struck by observing how small a proportion these pleasures bear to the pains, toils and anxious cares with which they have been sought? Were they our great good, surely they would not have been given with so sparing a hand. After all man's wearying sacrifices, what transient sensual gratification does he procure! After such prodigal expenditure of energy and thought, what does he actually gain! He succeeds imperfectly, in fencing off the ills to which his animal nature is exposed. Negative good is the chief result of most of the arts of life. It is not to enjoy, so much as to escape suffering, that man builds houses, weaves raiment, tills the fields, traverses the sea. And after all, how much must he endure, and how slightly can he be satisfied at the best! He shields the frail body for a few years amidst frequent visitations of disease; and at last life, which has been a continual battle, goes out in the brief agony of death. Does this look as if animal good were the prime purpose of man's being?

No creature works like man for the body, and no creature perhaps enjoys so little, so far as the mere body is concerned. Take for illustration the vast majority of the labouring classes in all nations. How do they toil from early dawn to dark, for six days out of seven, in cold and heat and frequent peril, to earn their coarse and scanty meals, and to find shelter and raiment—which, however they may ward off suffering, give slight positive pleasure to the sense of beauty or refined taste. Or take the case of merchants and traders, confined to counting-rooms by day, disturbed by cares at night, watching the vicissitudes of climate, the fluctuations of business, the caprices of popular fashion. Balance against their exertions the amount of mere animal pleasure yielded by all refinements, indulgencies and comforts which wealth can command, and answer, to which side the scale inclines. When we think of the endless toil out of doors, and the endless toil within, to keep up our common domestic establishments, the price which we pay for bodily existence appears to be enormous. How striking is the contrast between the inferior animals and men in this respect! As in the summer we watch countless insects flying from flower to flower, sipping their sweets, finding in every field a feast outspread, without one care of their own, extracting honey, not at a hurried meal, but through sunny hours and days, we may well feel that, so far as sensual pleasure goes, the moth is more privileged than the man. And so when we observe flocks and herds straying at will over verdant pastures, cropping their delicious food from morning till night, their very work their joy, they seem greatly to excel in animal gratification the drudging and exhausted husband-men,—who, with few intervals of rest or pleasure, enrich these very fields in which the care-free cattle graze, and then fill for them the farmyard and the barn with winter's food.

Nor is it clear that Civilization lightens man's burdens. Our Race has been toiling for ages to make the earth an animal paradise. But whether, after all improvements in the arts, we enjoy more than did our rude ancestors, may be fairly questioned. For Civilization, by increasing wants, has increased the modes of drudgery and care ; and by multiplying comforts more than habits of self-command, has intensified susceptibility to pain, converted petty privation into serious annoyance, and visited us with new and sore diseases. When thus we balance man's toils and enjoyments, we must admit that animal good is too limited, short-lived and unsatisfying, to be regarded as the Supreme End of life.

4. I pass to another view, teaching the same lesson, in a far more impressive way. Look round on this material world, which on all sides is ministering to us. Does it teach that the great purpose of Man's being is animal good? "What a vast machinery," it is sometimes said, "is kept in motion to sustain and comfort the animal creation." Undoubtedly this is one among countless purposes of the Universe. But surely it is not the great purpose, as respects mankind. This we infer, not only from the limited ministrations of Nature, but from its frequent hostile agency. How fearful, as well as

how benignant, an aspect does Creation wear! Behold the sun, the most·beneficent agent in our system. Does he not send scorching beams, breeding fever in summer, and such scanty rays in winter as to expose us to piercing frost? Does he not raise, together with salutary exhalations, deadly effluvia? Does he not at one time gather dense clouds which, precipitated in storms, prostrate in a day the labours of a season, and at another parch and wither vast regions with drought?

The great laws of Nature, in their general operations, are, indeed, beneficial; and the more largely they are explored, the more they attest a Good Creator. But who that contemplates the awful powers of the material world, as revealed in tempests, lightnings, earthquakes, volcanoes and wrathful oceans swept by whirlwinds, can think of this earth as having no higher use than to supply man's animal wants? What is a large part of man's existence but a ceaseless struggle with the destructive elements of Nature! What dangerous friends are even her most common gifts! The fire, by which we subdue the minerals and cheer our homes, perpetually threatens us with ruin. We must hem it in with walls of stone and iron, lest conflagration seize upon our dwellings, sweep through our streets, and reduce our whole substance and the gains of generations to ashes in an hour. We must battle even with hosts of insects for our harvests and our fruits, and thus fight an endless strife for daily bread. We talk of Nature as our Friend. Were not her mighty forces meant as plainly to oppose as to befriend us? Does not Nature bear evident marks of being planned to rouse man to heroic energy, by summoning us to conflict? How can one bear even to hear Nature called a "machine," as if it were a mill revolving for man's material uses? Its immense and tremendous energies, its floods of light, its hosts of stars, its unfathomable mysteries; are these meant only to give animal delight? Are they not manifestly designed rather to rouse far-reaching thought, to awaken profound awe, to inspire dauntless courage, and bring us into active concert with a Will infinitely transcending all material forces combined?

How different is the impression which Nature makes upon a thoughtful mind from that of dead "machinery"! In aspects of ineffable beauty and grandeur, it opens before us depth beyond depth, and touches inward springs of joy, gratitude and benevolence, which are as exhaustless as its own overflowing Life. For a Spirit of Power and Love breathes through, blends with, harmonizes and quickens this exquisitely ordered whole, with which we feel our own Spirits to be akin, by affinity and fellowship!

5. Such is the great lesson taught by Nature. And we may learn the same truth, that man is

made for a higher End, when we profoundly study
the very City, of which the first impression is that
it is a collection of beings brought together for
the purpose of ministering to one another's animal
life. What a monument is a City to the immortal
energies of the Human Mind; and what a witness
to man's Spiritual Destiny! When we gaze around
upon its stately structures for public and private
use; when we observe how the shapeless rocks, hewn
from the quarry, have been reared into edifices of
beautiful proportion and imposing grandeur; when
we notice the various technic arts which imitate
the creative powers of Nature, and elaborate the
rude materials into graceful forms adapted to social
refinement, can we help feeling that Man is a being,
whom the Inspiration of God welcomes to be a
Co-Creator with Himself? And when we enter the
houses which are so densely crowded together, what
do we find? Are they mere contrivances for safety
and shelter? Do we not instantly meet with countless provisions for higher tastes than mere animal
enjoyment—tastes which belong to Spiritual Beings,
who delight to sympathize in beauty, order, and
harmony? These pictures on the walls, were they
meant merely to gratify the sense of sight by colour?
Do they not breathe with grace, loveliness, and
dignity? Here may be the countenance of one
associated in our thoughts with years of unbroken
friendship, and hopes of a better world. There may

be the portrait of some heroic character, or the represented scene of some heroic enterprise, that reminds us how life, and all life's blessings, have been gladly cast away for truth, for country and for God. One such picture, in one house, is proof enough of Man's Spiritual Vocation!

But again I ask, what is the End of a human habitation? Is it merely a place wherein fellow-mortals meet to eat, drink and sleep securely beneath a roof? A house is reared to be a HOME,—the centre where a Family may gather into one; to be a serene retreat, where the tenderest affections may find rest; that within its walls love may have a dwelling-place, and the charities of life gain ample scope and happiness; that parents and children may there press one another heart to heart; that sorrows and joys may be freely shared in confidence; that troubled spirits may disburden themselves and be blessed with pardon and peace; and, in a word, that the great work of training human beings for the duties of the present life, and the perfection of another, may be begun and carried on. These are the True End of a human dwelling. As we pass through the streets of a City, what a thought of undying interest it is, that within these numberless homes are rich romances of domestic life—hearths, round which are gathered at evening the members of a family scattered by day, husbands and wives, parents and children, brethren and sisters,—

the sick and suffering nursed by the strong, the aged waited on by the respectful assiduity of the young,— amidst all the sympathies, labours, hopes, joys, sorrows, of disinterested love! In a City do we behold then only the signs of a being created for bodily and transitory good?

Moreover, among buildings destined for earthly uses, do we not observe churches with spires pointing towards the heavens; schools for the training of the young; public libraries stored with the wisdom of ages, and collections of books which welcome us to communion with sages, legislators, philosophers, historians and poets of all times and lands; museums of science, galleries of art, hospitals, asylums, all bearing witness that Man's End is to be a member of Society, to advance his Race, and to transform Humanity into the Kingdom of God, and thus prepare, by beauty and beneficence on earth, for the higher activities and joys of the Spiritual World?

II.—From this survey of man's animal nature I have shown that the End of Life is *not* mere activity upon the outward world. As a necessary consequence, I proceed to observe, that the great Work of Life is an inward one. This is our next position. Man's true Vocation may be defined to be Spiritual, as distinguished from a merely animal one.

1. Man has a Spiritual Nature. The Soul is created to look beyond and above all material things.

I begin with an obvious, yet all-convincing confirmation of this truth. In the Soul we find principles which enable us, and we might say compel us, to discover within Matter itself, the signs of an *infinitely* Higher Being. Is Matter a barrier which the Spirit cannot pass, beyond which all is darkness? How easily it scales this wall. In Nature everywhere it beholds witnesses of Supernatural Power. God! GOD! is the glorious Idea, that beams in splendour from all creation. In the heavens the Soul beholds an emblem of His Infinity. In the connexion and harmony of Nature it recognizes the type of His Unity. The Universe, vast, beautiful, magnificent as it is, cannot content the Soul, but rouses it to more majestic thoughts. The wider view it takes of what is material, the more impatient it becomes of all material bonds. The sublimer the prospects which are opened by the Universe, the more the Spirit is impelled to ascend to a still Sublimer Being. For ever it aspires towards an Infinite and Immutable One, as the ground of all finite and mutable existences. It can rest in His Omnipotence alone as the source, centre, sustainer, determiner of all forces.

How signally has God imprinted on us the End of our being in giving us this central impulse towards Himself! Why is it that this grandest thought in the Universe, that the Idea of this PERFECT BEING, dawns on the human mind? If

Man were made to find his chief good within the
compass of material nature, why does the Infinite
Spirit shine upon us throughout all Nature? The
Idea of God! Pause for a moment, and apprehend its grandeur. All other science fades into
insignificance before its majesty. The treasures of
all worlds are poor in contrast. This Idea, brightened
and unfolded till it becomes real to us, is as a new
Sun kindled within. From it a new Light streams
over and through the Universe. By the transforming power of this one Idea, all things become *new*.
The Idea of God! It is an exhaustless spring of
energy against weakness, of peace amid vicissitude,
of courage to do and suffer, of undying hope, of
immortal life. The cynic may speak contemptuously
of Human Nature; and the contemptible character
of the world's ordinary principles, maxims and feelings cannot well be exaggerated. But a being who
can think the Thought of God, be he ever so fallen,
is by that single power exalted to a Good, beyond
all natural good. Plainly such an Idea cannot have
been given for no End. It is the seal of a Heavenly
Destiny. It is the authentic handwriting of God
upon the Soul, revealing that man's true End is a
growing likeness in Spirit to Himself.

2. I proceed to another proof that the Soul was
created to look beyond and above all material interests. What is the great *motive* that prompts man
to the study of Nature? We know what intense

labour has been given to this pursuit. Now what has stirred Man to observe the sky, earth, atmosphere, plants, animals—in a word, all orders of creatures? Why did Newton concentrate his vast intellect upon determining the motions of the Universe? Why did Linnæus expend a life of toil in exploring the animal and vegetable kingdoms? Why have so many naturalists foregone the ease and security of civilized society, and plunged into savage forests, to note the habits of birds and insects, or to discover new minerals and plants? Has the great aim of these natural philosophers been to multiply the means of outward good? No! The unconquerable thirst for knowledge, for wide views, for a comprehension of the Order and Beauty of Creation as a whole:—this it is that has driven them into solitudes and deserts, and compelled them to bend every energy, at cost of utmost sacrifice, to the work of interpreting the secrets of nature. Truth! Truth has been the Divinity they have worshipped. The great men of science, so far from caring for the body, have cheerfully worn it out in daily and nightly study, have condemned it to exposure, fatigue, suffering, coarse raiment and scanty fare, and have died in poverty, that the Soul might live in the light of Truth. How many such glorious martyrs have left their record in the history of science! What, I repeat, has thus fired the Soul of the natural philosopher? It has been the quenchless desire to penetrate beyond what is visible to hidden Causes, to discover the great Laws which pervade and govern all material movements, to trace out Unity and Harmony in the apparently complex confusion of the Universe. This has been his inspiring aim.

Who does not behold a glorious signature of the End of the Human Soul in this hunger and thirst for Truth? Nor let it be said that I have been speaking of the experience of a few gifted men only, which proves nothing as to the purpose for which the Race was made. The distinctions among classes of men are far less than we suppose. The profoundest philosopher differs in degree only, not in kind, from the most uncultivated boor. Every man, however narrow his sphere, is daily putting forth in that very sphere the faculties which the philosopher exerts in his sublime pursuits. Every man has a love of truth, as Truth. And the zeal with which our lecture-rooms through cities, towns and villages, are weekly thronged by multitudes, not a few of whom have spent the day in manual toil, but who forget fatigue in the reception of new light and in the joy of mental refreshment, is a testimony to the Spiritual End for which the whole race was formed, as well as a cheering omen of the brighter social state which must surely come.

3. In the preceding remarks we have seen that Mind, in the very study of Matter, looks beyond it,

and seeks a Spiritual Good. I next observe that the Human Intellect is not confined to these branches of study, but everywhere manifests a tendency to higher investigations. The greatest minds, in all lands and ages, have given themselves to a profound study of the Spirit itself. And this is another striking proof, that we are created to look above everything outward to a Spiritual End. Vast as has been the amount of thought bestowed upon the material Universe, man's highest energy, through all generations, has been devoted to exploring the world within. The human mind has turned from all things, however wonderful and beautiful abroad, upon itself as the most interesting object of thought. And it has found within itself, in its original powers and affections, in its primitive intuitions and its growing acquirements, in its wonderful union of dependence and freedom, inexhaustible mysteries and problems which ages have failed to solve. The studies of Philosophy bear peculiar testimony to the grandeur of our Spiritual Nature. And they prove that the culture of this Spirit is the great work of life. The Philosopher, in studying the Mind, has found there not merely impressions received through the senses from the ever-changing world around, but immutable Principles which are essential elements of the Mind itself. He has found there Ideas of the Right, of the Good, of the First Cause, of Infinity, of Disinterested Love, of Moral Freedom, of Accountable-

ness—Ideas, which bear on them the stamp of
Universality and Eternity, which are not arbitrary,
local, transitory conceptions, but which belong essentially to All Intelligent Natures, and bring us into
communion with the highest orders of being.   Whilst
all around man is mutable, he has found unchangeable elements, convictions of Everlasting Truth in
the Human Soul.

The Philosopher, indeed, in studying the Soul,
has not only discerned that it is distinguished
from the fluctuating forms of matter, by its power
of apprehending Immutable Principles.   But he
has often been led to question whether anything
really exists in the Universe, beyond Mind and
Spirit; whether matter and the body have any substantial being; whether apparently external nature
be not an actual creation of our own thought; or,
in other words, whether, in believing in an outward
world, we do anything more than ascribe reality to
our own conceptions.   Thus from the very dawn
of Philosophy there have been Schools, which have
held that the Material Universe has no existence
but in the Mind, that thinks it.   I am far from
assenting to these speculations.   But I recur to
them with pleasure, as indicating how readily the
Soul passes above matter, and as manifesting man's
consciousness of the grandeur of his Spiritual Nature.
Let me add, that whilst rejecting this doctrine as
a whole, I receive an important part of it as un-

doubtedly true. I do not say that the world exists in our thoughts *only*. But I do say that it derives its most interesting properties from the Mind which contemplates it. For example, the forms of outward objects have doubtless actual existence; but they owe their Beauty—that mysterious charm—to thoughts and feelings which we blend with them, and of which they are but the reflected image. The very spot which is to one man a Paradise from the holy or happy thoughts, which he has associated with it, may be to another a desert. The glory that crowns the outward world is but a radiance streaming from ourselves. How much of the interest of the creation lies in the marks of Power and Beneficent Design, which apparently pervade it! But power and design are spiritual attributes, made known to us only by what passes within our own minds. So that from the Spirit spring the great Ideas which transform the Universe to us into the Symbol of the Living God. May we not be sure then that the Spirit was made for a Spiritual End, transcending all good which the Universe can bestow?

4. As another proof of the same doctrine, that man's End is a Spiritual one, let me ask you next to turn your thoughts to a most remarkable tendency of Human Nature. I refer to man's power of conceiving of more Perfect Beauty than exists within the limits of actual experience. Philosophers denote

this power by the word Imagination. This term to many suggests a faculty, that exaggerates or distorts reality, that feeds on dreams, and wastes itself on impracticable visions. Were these the true workings of the Imagination, instead of being its excesses, I should still think them indications of a being who has a sublime destiny to fulfil. The reveries of youth, in which so much energy is wasted, are the yearnings of a Spirit made for what it has not found but must for ever seek as an Ideal. It is not the proper use of the Imagination, however, to lose itself in dreams. This power, when acting, as it always should act, in unison with the Moral Principle, is a Divine Witness to the Spiritual End of human nature. Imagination passes beyond the transient and the bounded. It delights to bring together, and to blend in just proportion, whatever is lovely in Nature and the Soul. It separates from the elements of good all admixtures of evil and deformity, and thus aspires to the conception of peerless excellence and Perfect Beauty. In the present feeble unfoldings of virtue and greatness in human nature, it recognizes the germs of celestial goodness, and catches glimpses of the angel form which man is one day to wear. Imagination thus exalts and refines whatever it touches. For ever it sees in the visible the type of the Invisible, and in the outward world an image of the Inward, thus bringing them into harmony, and throwing added brightness over both. All things which it looks upon reveal a Being higher than themselves. Perfection! This is the vital air and element in which the Imagination breathes and lives. What a celestial power! What a testimony to the End of our being! Whence comes this tendency in human thought towards the Perfect, if man be not born for a progress which can never end?

This principle of Imagination—this desire for unattained good—this delight in consummate forms of beauty and happiness, is not confined to a favoured few. It is the fountain-head of the restless strivings of human life in every department. It is the soul of all great enterprise, though, when disjoined from the moral nature, and impelled by self-will, it may expend itself in destructive schemes of ambition. Above all, Imagination inspires the Poets, whose works have been the solace and encouragement of all nations through all stages of society. I am aware that some persons, when they hear Poetry thus spoken of, by a religious teacher, as one of the signs of man's being created to look above outward things, are tempted to think that he is throwing an air of fiction over reality. They want facts, they say, not fancy. I too prize facts, and am adducing nothing else. It is a fact—who can deny it?—that Poetry exists, and has existed among all people, savage and civilized. Its seeds are sown so plentifully in all human souls, that to overlook the beauty into which they bloom, is to close our eyes upon one of the most ennobling views of human nature. It is a fact, though many seem never to recognize it, that whole books of the Old Testament are Poems, whose sublime strains of piety and prophecy have thrilled and still thrill innumerable hearts. It is a fact, that in all nations religion and patriotism have spoken first in the language of Poetry; and that in most nations, Poetical Genius has been regarded as an Inspiration, and its works have been ranked amongst the most precious bequests of past ages. These are facts, attested by all history. And when we consider that the highest office of Poetry is thus to satisfy the aspirations of the Soul for the Perfect, and to create more attractive and commanding forms of heavenly virtue than meet our eyes, how can we fail to see in it the indication that man is made for a Spiritual End?

5. I proceed to another view, giving complete confirmation to this truth of man's Spiritual Destiny. Let me ask you to consider what form of human character it is, that our nature impels us to regard with the most fervent admiration? What peculiarly excites our reverence for our fellow-beings? Whose are the names which we pronounce in terms of the most affectionate homage? Who are the men in whom Human Nature seems to be

manifested in its brightest glory, who appear best to have fulfilled its End? In answering these questions, we shall find that the individuals, who have left enduring traces of themselves in the memories and hearts of their fellows, and who are thought of with a spontaneous overflow of love and honour, are those who have made the greatest sacrifices of outward good for inward principle, for truth, humanity, religion, patriotism and freedom. It is not to those who have laboured for the body, but to those who have offered it up in virtuous toil, or martyrdom; it is not to those who have accumulated outward good, but to those who have parted with it most freely; not to those who have watched over and kept their lives, but to those who have cheerfully given them away; that the tribute of reverence and joyful commemoration has been paid. In dramas, romances, histories and biographies, the Heroic Sufferer for principle and generous affection wins the love of all uncorrupted hearts.

Contempt of all outward things, which come in competition with duty, fulfils the Ideal of human greatness. This conviction, that readiness to sacrifice life's highest material good and life itself, is essential to the elevation of Human Nature, is no illusion of ardent youth, nor outburst of blind enthusiasm. It does not yield to growing wisdom. It is confirmed by all experience. It is sanctioned by conscience—that universal and eternal lawgiver

—whose chief dictate is, that everything must be
yielded up for the Right. What a testimony have
we here, that we were created to look above and
beyond animal existence! Whilst we are impelled
by urgent desires and needs to labour for outward
means of good, yet our highest love and admiration
are given to those who joyfully renounce them all.
For such we rear our stateliest monuments. Wisdom,
Genius, and the People's heart preserve and hallow
the memory of such Heroes. In history and song,
in painting and sculpture, we keep alive their names
and images. Even superstition, in treasuring up
the relics of Martyrs, as endowed with miraculous
power, is a witness to the glory of renouncing the
body, and consecrating it to the cause of Truth and
Right. Are we not surely made then to look above
all outward things, and seek a Spiritual End?

6. I shall adduce but one proof more of man's
Spiritual Vocation. It is found in the principle of
Faith that aspires after an Immortal Life. I call
this Faith a natural principle, not only because it
has been manifested through all nations, and is co-
existent with the human race, but because it has its
roots in all man's highest faculties and affections.
Faith in Immortality is but the supreme form of
foresight and of hope. Who does not exercise these
principles every hour? But what is there to bound
their range within the future of this world? Have
not hope and foresight an innate energy, impelling

them towards Eternity, which cannot be arrested by the tomb? Faith in the Future Life is natural; for it springs necessarily from the very Ideas of God and Duty—Ideas the most congenial and native to the soul! The Perfection of God, His Eternal Power and Goodness, in proportion as they become real to us, give birth to the assured hope of receiving a higher life from His hand than the present; and the consciousness of Duty necessarily awakens an anticipation of equitable retribution, and of continued progress for all seekers of virtue. It is impossible that a being, capable of these great thoughts, should be pent up within a perishable body, or limited in development to this brief life. Accordingly there is a deep want in our nature, to which no change of outward circumstance brings relief; that increases with civilization, refinement, knowledge and our power over the natural world; that adds immeasurably to the weight of disappointment and calamity; that cries out for and unweariedly seeks a higher mode of being. To many men, indeed, the Future Life becomes so real and so near, as to destroy their interest in the present. The actual life fades before the light of Immortality, as tapers pale before the sun. Faith becomes too vivid to allow a just concern for the events of this transient world. Is not a being, gifted with such foresight and sublime power of hope, manifestly created to live and work, and for ever aspire towards a Spiritual End?

The doctrine of this discourse is no barren speculation, but a practical truth, bearing directly on
active life, and affecting our whole happiness here
and hereafter. It seems to need a specially earnest
exposition at the present day, not because it is
denied, but because it is thrown out of sight in
the vehemence of worldly pursuits. In every age
some element of our nature is brought out dispro-
portionately, and exerts too exclusive a control.
At present the Material Principle is unfolded with
such augmented power, that the true balance between man's Spiritual and Animal nature is disturbed, if not destroyed. We have arrived at a
period of civilization when man's mastery over outward forces begins to be understood. This knowledge of the laws of the material world has received
mighty impulses and practical applications, never
conceived of before. Consequently the prospect of
physical comfort and enjoyment, once confined to
the few, is now thrown open to all. Unhappily,
no proportionate new light has been cast upon the
capacities and energies of the Spirit. The true
doctrine seems to be dying out—that man's elevation and happiness consist and can be found
only in strength of Soul, in clear conceptions and
deep convictions of Everlasting Truth, in calm
reliance upon God and Duty, in stern resolve of
cleaving to the Right, in self-possession under every
change, in self-conquest amidst all temptation, in

energy to do or suffer whatever may be imposed by Conscience, in disinterested and fearless self-consecration to whatever good work we may be appointed by Providence.

This Spiritual Dominion, this Kingdom of Heaven within the Soul, alone endures, alone gives dignity and peace. And yet with what scepticism, indifference, and even scorn, is such a doctrine heard in this age of materialism, of machinery and of proud trust in man's dominion over nature! Still, let the true doctrine be preached in full confidence that what is so confirmed by the attestations of conscience, in all ages, cannot but find response. Man's Spiritual Nature is no dream of theologians to vanish before the light of Natural Science. It is the grandest Reality on earth. Everything here but the Soul of Man is a passing shadow. The only enduring Substance is within. When shall we awake to the sublime greatness, the perils, the accountableness, and the glorious destinies of the Immortal Soul? O! for a voice of power to arouse the Human Spirit from its death in life of animality, to quicken it with a fit consciousness of its own nature, to lift it to an adequate comprehension of the purposes for which the sublime thoughts of God, of Duty, of Disinterested Love, of Heaven, are opened within! In what a vain show we walk, while we toil without ceasing for the perishable, and remain blind and dead to the Everlasting, the Perfect and the Divine!

VIII.

THE PERFECTING POWER

OF RELIGION.

THE PERFECTING POWER
OF RELIGION.

Be ye therefore Perfect, even as your Father which is in heaven is Perfect.—MATTHEW V. 48.

By what influence is Religion our Supreme Good? Much mystery would be removed from the Religious Life, and men would seek it more wisely and efficiently, if they understood with more precision the true Blessedness which it confers. On this point my views may be expressed in a few words. My belief is that the Supreme Good of an intelligent and moral being is the Perfection of its Nature. Nothing gives what is worthy of being considered Happiness, and nothing is of enduring benefit, unless it exalts us to that Excellence for which God designs us. Religion is the spring of peace and joy as the Inspirer of Universal Virtue,—as pre-eminently a *quickening* principle, giving life and energy to the Intellect and the Heart, fortifying Conscience, and animating it with an unconquerable purpose of duty, awakening Love in its purest and most disinterested forms, raising Thought to its highest objects, and thus training our whole being to that fulness, harmony and beauty, the union of which constitutes Perfection.

Religion gives Happiness by its inward influence. Too many ascribe to it a different operation. They regard it as a worship of God, in order to win his favour. They imagine that it serves and saves us by conciliating our Maker, by its effect upon another, not upon ourselves; by its procuring good from abroad, not by its unfolding and elevating our own souls. Few, indeed, understand how essential is the growth of their own highest affections and energies,—that without this nothing can do them good, and that to promote this is the great function of religion.

This Truth is worthy of development. Let me re-state it so that it may be fully understood. I affirm, then, that the great office of religion is to call forth, elevate and purify the Spirit of Man, and thus to conform it to its Divine Original. I know no other way in which Religion is to promote our Happiness; for I know no Happiness but that of a good, wise, upright, firm, powerful, disinterested, elevated Character. I look to religion for blessings, because it includes and promotes Universal Excellence, brings the soul into health and concord, enlarges it, unfolds it in due proportions, and exalts it to the beauty and power for which it was created. It is the office of religion, I repeat once more, to call forth the *whole* Spirit of

Man, the Intellect, the Conscience, the Affections, the Will; to awaken Energy and holy purpose; to inspire a calm and rational, yet a profound love of Truth and Goodness, against which all powers of the universe will be impotent. Did I not hope for this quickening influence from religion, I could not speak of it as the Supreme Good. For our Supreme Good is the Perfection of our being; and nothing which does not involve and promote this deserves the name.

It is said, I know, that our Happiness comes from God, not from ourselves. And this language, justly interpreted, conveys a great truth. God is the only fountain of Blessedness. But from the Nature of things, and from His own Perfection, He makes beings blessed through and according to the capacities with which He endows them, and in no other way. I can expect from my Creator no Happiness but one proportioned to my Nature. And what is my Nature? I answer that pre-eminently I am a Moral Being. I have a sense of duty, a perception of virtue, an inward voice commanding me with Divine Authority to reverence Right in every act, to eradicate all evil from my heart and life, and to advance towards that Perfection of which I catch a glimpse, but which shines in full glory far before me. Now I affirm that the proper Blessedness of such a being, that for which I was made, consists in conforming myself to this principle of Rectitude. I am not more conscious that I live, than I am that the Moral Principle is given to be the governing power of my nature; and that in resisting it, or in abandoning it to the sway of the passions, I do and must forfeit the proper good of my being. No other real good is left. In resisting it, I arm against myself, and turn into a foe the divinest power of my soul; carry on a perpetual war in my own breast, and 'incur that severest suffering in the universe, self-rebuke. These remarks will show in what sense we are to believe that God gives us Happiness. He gives it to us through ourselves, through the improvement of our whole nature, and in no other way. And the knowledge, love and service of God, or religion, is the means of Supreme Good, because it is the great quickening principle by which our being is perfected.

We are to be made happy then—let us never forget it—by what we ARE, not by what we *have*, by the purity and power of our own minds, and not by what is given us from abroad. We are too apt with insane eagerness to gather round ourselves defences and means of enjoyment, whilst the mind is left uneducated, and the character untrained. We are too apt to use religion itself as a kind of outward charm, and to expect that it will make us happy by some mysterious agency, instead of looking to it as the Central, Life-giving

Principle, and as the great refiner and purifier of the Soul.

I.—Am I asked how Religion is the impelling power towards Perfection, and how, in strengthening it, we fortify every noble principle? I will give a few answers drawn, in the first instance, from our Moral Nature.

1. Religion gives infinite worth to Conscience. Religion does not create Conscience. For whether I am a religious man or not, I shall, as a man, still have some sense of duty, and of the distinctions between good and evil. But this Moral Principle lacks life, when not quickened and sustained by confidence in a Righteous God. Conscience is not equal of itself to the work of withstanding temptation, and raising us to our true dignity. The passions are too strong. Do not all feel this to be true? Persuade a man that no Higher Authority in the Universe, than his own conscience, enjoins on him self-restraint, cut him off from any Higher Lawgiver and Judge than his own reason, and probably he will become enslaved to some lower principle. The conscience was never intended to govern alone. It was made to derive dominion from a conscious union with a Supreme Being. And this Supreme Being is revealed to us by religion. Religion is faith in an Infinite Creator, who delights in and enjoins that Rectitude which conscience commands us to seek. This

conviction gives a Divine Sanction to duty. From religion I learn that my Idea of Right is not an individual, private, personal conviction, but that it is derived from the Universal Parent; that it is His Inspiration; that it is not a lonely voice in my own soul, but the word of the Infinite Will. Now I see that Goodness is not merely a law of my own mind, but the Supreme Law of the Universe, that all intelligent beings are subject to it, that all creation conspires to fulfil it. Without this faith in a Holy God, duty would be but a whisper in my breast. With Him it comes in a voice louder than all thunders. Without a consciousness of God, I might hope to win happiness in spite of the violation of the law of Rectitude. Now I know that it would be more rational to seek happiness on the rack or in the furnace, than in wrong-doing. All Nature now becomes to me the preacher of righteousness; for the heavens and the earth, the sunshine and storms, in their very Order, reveal an Almighty Power, who is pledged to the support of virtue and to the suppression of sin. Without a God, there would be no other Inspector of my motives, thoughts, desires and purposes, than my own soul; and I might succeed in disguising from myself, and hiding from others, inward impurity and deformity. But now a Light more piercing than a thousand suns, and veiled by no cloud nor night, shines full upon me; and I feel that my most secret purposes lie bare before Infinite Purity. Who does not recognize the authority added to conscience, the sanction given to duty, by this confidence in an Almighty Lawgiver, and an Ever-present Judge, whose law and supreme delight are the Moral Perfection of His children.

2. In another view, Religion is the great spring of Moral improvement. This confidence in God alone gives the hope of reaching Perfection. Hope inspires energy. But without trust in God I have no sufficient hope to excite and sustain persevering efforts after excellence. True, there are other aids of virtue besides religion,—the approbation and rebukes of conscience, the esteem and honour of fellow-beings, the present recompenses of upright-ness and charity. But that watchful discipline over the inmost thoughts and motives, that aspiration after disinterestedness and inward purity, that scorn of suffering in the way of well-doing, that prefer-ence of the soul's health and progress to outward interests, that conflict with absorbing self-love,—all of which are so essential to eminence and perma-nence of Rectitude,—come not from ourselves. They demand continual, fresh supplies of Divine Inspira-tion. So tremendous is the power of passion, so subtle is temptation, so contagious is the influence of example, that a man, conscious of no Higher Power than his own, and expecting no improvement but such as he can compass by his unaided will,

might well despair of resisting the combined powers
of evil. An Infinite Motive is needed to quicken
us in this never-ending war with selfishness and
the world. And where is such a motive to be found,
if we believe in no Everlasting Friend of goodness,
and in no Future Life where our present spiritual
growth will be crowned with Perfection?

Take away the prophetic hopes of religion, and my
nature is full of discouraging contradictions. I see
and approve the good, and resolve on amendment and
progress. I have conceptions of excellence, which
I burn to make real in character and deed. But
the weight of mortality depresses the spirit to the
dust; resistless currents are hurrying down my
nature to indulgence; there is a tendency to excess
in every passion and impulse; and sensuality
and sloth perpetually thwart the upward efforts
of the moral nature. Is there in the universe no
Power of Good to overcome evil higher than I am
conscious of in my own breast? How then can I
ever realize that Ideal of excellence which shines
before me? Then can I attain at best but to a
low virtue. When I consider too—as without religious faith I must—that even this low virtue will
soon pass from me, that I have no power to preserve
it beyond the grave, that every high aspiration,
benevolent sympathy and upright energy is to
perish with the body, what motive remains sufficient to quicken me in becoming better? Hope is

the gift of religion. Religion teaches not only that there is an Infinite Lawgiver, but an Infinite Inspirer of virtue. It teaches us that God delights to perfect His intelligent offspring; that He has made us for the very end of imparting to us His own Spirit; and that there are no bounds to this communication of His Life. It teaches us that we are subjected to temptations, both within and without, as a trial to awaken effort, to remind us of our need of aid, and to prepare us for a higher mode of spiritual being. It teaches us that the Ever-Living has infinite love for each human soul, and that present virtue is but the germ of an ever-growing goodness. According to religion no effort can be lost. What we gain here we shall carry with us hereafter. Death will be a *birth* into a new life. Sprung from an Eternal Parent, surely as God lives we are to live for ever. Our connexion with the Eternal One gives us a hold on all future ages. In Him there is a power to uphold and carry us forward through a Boundless Universe, and without end. Believing in the All-good, I feel that the Perfection of my own Spirit is no dream; that it may become a reality; that this Spirit may actually be pure, powerful, bright and blessed as an angel's; that, if faithful to the laws of the Religious Life, I shall conquer not only death, but what is so much more terrible than death, the power of moral evil! Believing in a Heavenly Father, I can set no bound to my hope

of what man is to become under the purifying influence of Jesus Christ and his religion. I anticipate that here on earth, perhaps at no distant
day, when Christianity shall be purified from its corruptions, that human character will rise to greater
dignity and beauty, than we can now conceive.
And when I look forward to the Future World, to
a succession of ages without end, I am overwhelmed
with a sense of impotence to conjecture to what
heights of power, love, happiness, a human being,
loyal to God and to duty, is destined to attain. The
most glowing language, in which genius and piety
have sought to shadow forth the felicities of man's
future being, seems but tame and inexpressive. Man,
improving for ever under the influences of the
Infinite and Immortal God, is assured of a destiny
as incomprehensible now as is God's own being.

3. I can offer but one other consideration to
show that Religion is the great spring of elevation in Character. It offers to us, for our veneration
and love, and perpetual intercourse, a Being whose
Character comprehends all venerable and lovely attributes; who reveals to us within Himself, without
spot or limit, that very Perfection of Goodness, after
which our moral nature impels us to aspire. We
all know the aid which the mind acquires from
communion with a human being of noble qualities;
how in admiring him it exalts itself; how his presence, voice, countenance, influence, lift it above its

ordinary tone. To contemplate and love excellence is to be inspired by it. Attachment to an excellent being is itself excellent, and conforms us to his image. Now religion places us in the presence of Infinite Purity. It raises the mind in meditation, gratitude, sympathy and filial awe to the Father of the Universe. It recognizes everywhere in creation the traces and radiant signatures of the Greatest and Best Mind. It teaches us to feel that a Higher than man's agency, a Grander than man's presence, for ever surrounds us. I know nothing but this conscious relationship with an Existence more exalted than our own that can truly elevate us. We suffer, and often deeply, by our intercourse with fellow-beings. Perpetually we are tempted to fall under the influence of lower feelings, till we become insensible to the reality and worth of our highest spiritual nature. But by feeling the Presence and the Perfection of our Spiritual Father, the consciousness of our own spiritual being brightens within us. Sentiments of love and veneration towards this Invisible Source of all spiritual good subdue the depressing influences of our material organization. Religion, where it becomes a Principle of Life, works a greater transformation in our existence, than would be wrought were a new eye given to us, by which we should behold ourselves surrounded with a higher race of Spiritual Beings, and thus should be enabled to enter into intimate intercourse

with them. In truth all other friendships are
powerless to exalt the character, or to give happiness, compared with this Divine Friendship which
is the very essence of the Religious Life.

II.—The doctrine that Religion can do us good,
only by refining and perfecting our Whole Being,
is of such great moment, that I proceed to illustrate it further. For I am satisfied that one cause
of the limited sway of religion is the narrow conception formed of its function. That religion is
a Universal Principle,—spreading its influence
through the whole being, developing every power
to a fulness which it could not otherwise attain,
diffusing inspiration through the Intellect, as well
as the Conscience and the Will, taking under its
purifying rule the Appetites and Passions as well
as the Affections, imparting fresh interest to common existence, exalting and expanding practical
energy, refining and adorning social manners, add-
ing cheerfulness as well as purity to friendly
intercourse, and blessing us only by this universally
enlivening agency,—this is a truth not yet understood as it should be. Hence to many, Religion,
instead of being thought of as comprehending
whatever is good, wise, energetic, beautiful, great
and happy in Human Nature, is a word of doubtful
import,—especially suggesting notions of restraint,
repression, narrowness of thought, exclusive feeling
and habitual gloom.

I could not commend the Religious Life, did I not view it in the broad light in which I am now attempting to place it. For nothing can make us truly happy but our Perfection. And the very idea of Perfection is, that the *whole* nature of a being is unfolded in due proportion, so that the highest and worthiest powers will hold ascendency, and all others, by acting in their true spheres, will fulfil the end for which they were given. Such Universal Development constitutes, as we all know, the health and beauty of the body. A man in whom a few organs only should grow, would be a monster. Even if this excess should occur in his noblest organs, as the head or the eye, we should still regard him as deformed. The body is a healthful and beautiful organization, only when the principle of life acts generously through all its parts, expanding all in a just degree, so that each contributes to the vigour and symmetry of the whole. Such an organization we call a Perfect Body. And so Perfection of Mind consists in well-proportioned activity and life, through *all* its faculties, affections, desires, powers, whereby they all grow up into one harmonious whole.

The prevalent error always has been, that men have confined their conceptions of religion too much to its *direct* agencies. They have supposed it to consist chiefly in immediate thoughts of God, in immediate addresses to Him, and in fervours of emotion called forth by immediate contemplation of His glory. Now religion so viewed cannot insure our highest happiness. I know, indeed, that these spiritual acts are often the most delightful of which our nature is capable. The pious man, when able to concentrate every energy of mind and heart upon the Infinite Goodness of his Creator, and to enter by faith and hope into communion with the Unseen and Everlasting World, has a foretaste of joy unspeakable and full of glory. But I need not tell you that this elevation of thought and feeling is not designed to be the ordinary state of even the most improved human beings. We were plainly not designed for this constant intense action of our spirits towards our Creator. No effort on our part can long sustain it. And were it sustained for a protracted period, it would end in the exhaustion and derangement of our faculties. Besides, there are not a few who seem constitutionally incapacitated for such ardour of religious emotion. If religion insured our happiness, then, only as giving us an immediate enjoyment of God, it would really contribute but little to our well-being,—the greater part of life being necessarily devoted to other duties and engagements, to intercourse with fellow-beings, to toils and relaxations, and to putting forth creative energy on the material world. We cannot live absorbed in the work of adoration. We cannot keep our minds perpetually bent upon one object. And the brighter that object the sooner are we dazzled and exhausted.

I am conscious that I was made for an endless variety of thoughts, interests, sympathies and occupations. I have curiosity impelling me to seek the new and explore the mysterious; the reasoning faculty prompting me to infer the unknown from the known, and to rise from particulars to general truths; imagination for ever surpassing the bounds of the real and the present; the love of beauty enjoying all harmonies; social affections, putting on a thousand forms according to the relations and characters of those around me; the senses, through which countless images and symbols of the material world rush in and throng my mind; and finally animal appetites compelling me to put forth energy upon material objects. Now all these principles and tendencies of my nature are various capacities of enjoyment, and all demand their proper forms of good. Nothing can make me truly happy but a Universal Principle, that watches over, protects, calls forth and gratifies in their due order all these various elements of my being. Such I hold to be the influence of religion; and it is through this function that it becomes our Supreme Good.

I insist the more on this, because religion has suffered from nothing so much as the false notion of its being an exclusive principle. Men in all ages have thought that they must sacrifice to religion some element of their nature. To cherish the Religious Principle, some have warred against their social affections, and have led solitary lives; some against their senses, and have abjured all pleasure in asceticism; some against reason, and have superstitiously feared to think; some against imagination, and have foolishly dreaded to read poetry or books of fiction; some against the political and patriotic principle, and have shrunk from public affairs: all apprehending that if they were to give free range to their natural emotions, their Religious Life would be chilled or extinguished. Thus the notion of hostility, between Religion and Human Nature, has in some form or other insinuated itself into believers of most different systems of faith. Now, in opposition to all such views, I would maintain, that the true office of religion is to bring out the *whole nature* of man in harmonious activity, and that, by thus developing it after a Divine Order, to show how divine a work Human Nature is, and for what Divine Happiness it is destined.

To understand better this office and agency of religion, let us observe that our nature is composed of Superior and Inferior powers. All these religion takes under its care, the lowest as well as the highest. But it promotes our happiness in an especial manner by enlivening and perfecting the highest first. And to this influence of religion the necessary limits of this discourse compel me to confine attention. These higher powers of human nature are commonly ranged under two classes, the Moral and the Rational—the first called Conscience, or the power of Rectitude ; the last called Intellect, or the power of knowing Truth. These being our highest powers, nothing can be plainer, as was argued under the former head of this discourse, than that our happiness depends upon their free and full development. The just view of religion, which I am anxious to present, is, that it is the great Principle by which these distinguishing powers of humanity are quickened and enlarged, and that in this way it chiefly promotes our happiness. Under the former head, I have shown how religion perfects our Moral Faculties by unfolding the Conscience. I pass now to the second class of our higher faculties, the Rational, and would briefly show that it is the office of religion to perfect the Intellect.

It is a painful reflection that as yet the Intellect is a source of but little happiness to the majority of mankind. In the vast multitudes, among all nations, it is doomed to inaction and lethargy. In the labouring classes of every land it is famished by want of education, oppressed by drudging toil and urgent necessities of the

animal nature, and darkened by countless prejudices and superstitions. And in all classes however cultivated, Intellect is too much the slave of the
senses and of selfish passions, and is yet to be
awakened to a consciousness of its real glory. To
religion I look as the power by which this divine
faculty is to be revealed and exalted to its true
felicity. Am I asked how religion acts so bene-
ficially upon the Intellect, I answer in various
ways, of which a few only can now be selected
for illustration.

1. Religion then is the great Inspirer of the
Intellect, in the first place, by exhibiting its essential grandeur, and by teaching it to reverence itself.
It is religion only that teaches us this reverence
for the Intellect. For it alone reveals to us the
connexion of the Intellect with God, its deriva-
tion from His Wisdom, its nearness to His Reason,
its capacity of everlasting reception of His Light
of Truth. Separated from God, I can regard my
intellect only as a power, which is to endure but
a brief span, and which can advance but little
beyond its present bounds. And when so viewed,
I am oppressed by the consciousness of the impotence
and insufficiency of human intelligence. There is
not a single object of my thought in regard to
which the unknown does not infinitely exceed what
I am able to know. The moment I would penetrate beneath the surface, whether of material things

or of spiritual beings, whether of the lifeless stone or of the thinking soul, I find a depth utterly unfathomable by my reason in this present stage of existence. And even within the narrow sphere of actual knowledge, errors constantly admonish me of my mental weakness. So that every act of my mind leads to most humbling and discouraging estimates of itself. I do not wonder that men of superior intelligence, but wanting in religious faith, have been led by a review of the extravagances and baffled efforts of the philosophic class, to treat with contempt all claims of human reason of attaining to truth. It is only as we apprehend our relationship to an All-wise God, that we can understand ourselves, and become to ourselves objects of awe and solemn interest. The human mind, regarded as the offspring of the Infinite Mind, consciously partakes of the grandeur of its source. Let me know that an Infinite Intelligence pervades the Universe, and I feel that intelligence without bounds may be possible also for myself. Let me further know that this Infinite Intelligence is the Parent of my mind, has an interest in it, watches over it and created it that it should unfold for ever, and partake more and more of His own Truth, and how can I but regard my intellect with veneration? Then I look abroad upon this vast creation, which before had discouraged me, with joy and hope; for I see in its very vastness only a wider field for intellectual culture. I cease to be depressed by learning slowly, if I am to learn for ever. Nor am I any longer cast down by difficulties in gaining truth; for the energy and hardihood of thought, acquired by struggling with obstacles and by a laborious training, are the best preparation for an endless progress. Religion thus reveals the grandeur, and still more the sacredness, of human intellect. For it shows that Reason is not figuratively but really a Divine Energy working in us. No other motive can have equal efficacy in teaching us to watch over and expand this heavenly gift. The power of this motive is but little known, because man's Living Relationship with God through the *vital influence* of religion has as yet been but faintly comprehended; and what has been called religion has too often tended to depress rather than to invigorate human reason.

2. In another way religion gives life to the Intellect, and converts its action into a means of joy. It communicates new interest to all objects of thought. Religion begins by revealing to us the most interesting Being in the Universe, whose Character is inexhaustible alike in its essential Perfection and in its endless Manifestations; and whose nearness to us, and constant Influence upon us, arrest the mind with intense admiration, such as all other beings cannot inspire. Nor is this all.

Religion reveals Creation to us as *vitally* connected with this Being of beings, the work of His incessant power, the object of His constant care, comprehended within His boundless goodness, and moved and guided by His influent energy. Thus it throws a new light over all existences, and invests them with a portion of the interest with which God Himself is regarded. Yes! All things within and around us, the earth, sea and heavens, our fellow-creatures and the material world, human nature and human history, all rise into a brighter glory, disclose profounder meanings, and attract the mind with a new charm, when once they are associated in our thoughts with the Infinite Mind. The Universe becomes an open book of Divine Wisdom. Nothing appears too small to become worthy of study, when we recognize that God has imprinted on it His Thought, and left within it some symbol of His own Perfection. All true Science is essentially religious. It springs from the intuition of Permanent and Universal Law in nature. And its end is to trace out connexions, dependencies, and harmonious laws throughout creation. It looks upon Nature as one vast system, as a complex whole, all parts of which are bound together and are co-working for the common good. Now these harmonies, connexions, general laws and common purposes are all the emanation and expression of a Supreme and Disposing Mind. They are Divine

Intelligence made visible. It is then the Intelligence pervading Nature that Science studies. Thus in all its discoveries it is virtually tracing out the method of Divine Reason, and, however unintentionally, it contributes to the glory of God's Revealed Truth. The tendencies of Science are all towards God. And consequently it can never be prosecuted so triumphantly and so joyfully, as when quickened and led by the living consciousness of Communion with the Infinite Mind.

3. This leads us to another view, showing us the influence of the Religious Principle in perfecting the Intellect. It favours that primary virtue of an intelligent being, fairness of mind, the honest disposition to receive light whencesoever it may come. This uprightness of judgment, impartiality in research and superiority to prejudice contributes more to the discovery of truth, and to real wisdom, than the most splendid genius or the most laborious acquirement. This simple sincerity is worth more than all books, teachers, colleges, and literary apparatus. No matter with what power of intellect a man may be gifted, no matter how extensive may be his means of knowledge, if he want candour, openness to conviction, readiness to see and acknowledge error, and above all reverence for Truth as sacred, his intellectual endowments will be used only to fortify himself in prejudice, to defend opinions which passion has recommended to

his intellect, or to invent doctrines which will best serve to build up his fame. The wildest theories, most ruinous projects, and most pernicious principles, have owed their origin to highly intellectual men. Now I know no influence like that of religion to form an upright mind. This influence it exerts, not only by inspiring us with that reverence for the intellect already spoken of, but also by awakening the conviction that the intellect is formed for continual progress toward Truth; and that, consequently, to chain it down to its present imperfect views, is to rob it of its destiny. Still more religion exerts this influence, by making us feel that we are carrying on our most private inquiries, reasonings, judgments, in the Presence of that God, who is Infinite Light, and whose Intelligence is Truth. It is the secrecy with which the mind prosecutes its researches, weighs evidence, and makes objections, that tempts us to shut our eyes to the light. But a consciousness of the Presence of God to the mind brings home to us our responsibility for our judgments as well as actions. The consciousness that His pure eye inspects us, compels us to inspect ourselves, and to guard jealously against every influence from abroad, or from our own passions, which may pervert the reason. Thus it makes luminous the intellect. Religion opens the mind to Truth; and Truth is the atmosphere wherein our rational nature becomes illumined and made fit to enter the world of perfect light.

4. This doctrine, that it is religion which chiefly quickens the Intellect and makes it a blessing, might be illustrated by a variety of considerations which it was my hope to place before you, but on which time is wanting to enlarge. I intended, for instance, to show that the principle of Universal Love, which is embraced in true religion, and is indeed its Essence, disposes the mind to the most enlarged thinking, and at the same time makes knowledge active and practical, thus converting it into Wisdom, by directing it to the promotion of the highest good in the service of mankind.

5. Again, I particularly intended to show that religion is a source of light to the Intellect by opening to it the highest order of truths, and thus introducing it to a Celestial Happiness. On this topic it might not be easy to avoid the charge of mysticism. I believe, however, and I wished to prove, that the highest truths are not those which we learn from abroad. No outward teaching can bestow them. They are unfolded from within, by our very progress in the Religious Life. New ideas of Perfection, new convictions of Immortality, a new consciousness of God, a new perception of our Spiritual Nature, come to us as revelations, and open upon us with a splendour which belongs not to this world. Thus we gain the power to look with deeper penetration

into human life, as well as into the universe. We read a wider significance in events. We attain to glimpses of the Infinite Mind and of a Future World, which, though we may not be able to define them in human speech, we yet know to correspond to Realities. Now this higher wisdom, whereby the Intellect anticipates the bright visions which await it in another life, comes only from the growth and dominant influence of the Religious Principle, by which we become transformed more and more into the likeness of God. So true is it that Religion makes Intellect a blessing, and an infinite blessing.

In this discourse I have thus aimed to show how Religion is our Supreme Good, by giving life and force to our highest powers, bringing them into the healthiest and most harmonious activity, and quickening us in the pursuit of Perfection. Earnestly do I insist that Religion blesses us by no mysterious agency in procuring the favour of an All-powerful Being who will do everything for us without our co-operation, but by unfolding that pure, firm, disinterested, lofty Character, and that large, just and wise Intelligence,—which conform us to the likeness of our Divine Parent, and best fit us to enjoy fellowship with Him, in His Natural Creation and in His Spiritual World. Religion welcomes us to be Perfect, as Our Father in Heaven is Perfect.

IX.

JESUS CHRIST THE BROTHER,

FRIEND AND SAVIOUR.

JESUS CHRIST THE BROTHER, FRIEND AND SAVIOUR.

Behold, I bring you good tidings of great joy, which shall be to all people. For unto you is born this day a Saviour, which is Christ the Lord. And this shall be a sign unto you; Ye shall find the babe wrapped in swaddling clothes, lying in a manger.—LUKE ii. 10, 11, 12.

CHRISTMAS has come once more—the day devoted by the large majority of Christians to the commemoration of the Nativity of the Saviour. In both hemispheres of our globe, and almost from pole to pole, the voice of thanksgiving to-day is lifted up, for the coming of Christ into the world. The appropriation of this day for a festival is not, indeed, a part of our religion. But it is natural, it is human,—when so many of our brethren are turning their hearts and thoughts to Bethlehem,—that we should repair thither with them to sympathize in their pious gratitude. Accordingly, this text has been chosen, as the guide of our morning meditations.

Why then should we feel "great joy," as in thought we gather around this "Babe" lying in the "Manger"? The question may be answered in various forms. Two views are suggested by the text, to which I shall ask in turn your attention. First, we should rejoice, because we have a Saviour, who was *born;* and secondly, because his birth was marked by conditions of singular *humiliation.* After considering these two points, I will close this discourse with unfolding the sense, in which, as it appears to me, this Babe, born in the Manger of Bethlehem, became and is a *Saviour.*

I.—It is a ground of great joy, I think, that we have a Saviour who was *born* to us,—that is a Saviour who appeared in *our own Nature.* You know it is the doctrine of many Christians—a doctrine supported apparently by the letter of various texts—that Jesus existed before his human birth. Now, I say, that it is cause of gratitude and joy, that he did not come to us in a pre-existent glory—that he did not descend from Heaven in the array of an archangel. It is matter of joy that our Deliverer was clothed with humanity. For this has brought him near us, and established a bond of sympathy which is inestimably precious.

Jesus, by his birth, was truly a *human being;* and in this we should rejoice. He was flesh of our flesh. He had our wants and desires, our hunger and thirst, our sensations of pleasure and pain, our natural passions. He was born of woman, was folded in a mother's arms, was nourished from a mother's breast; and he felt the gratitude, the tenderness of a son. He bore the relations of human life towards kindred, neighbours and friends. He grew up amidst the labours of mortal men, ate the bread of his own earnings, and was acquainted by experience with the hardships to which the multitude of mankind are exposed. He was thus actually one of our race, a Brother of the great Human Family. And we have reason to rejoice that such a Deliverer was sent to us. I am not prepared to say that the benefit of such an appointment is, that it gives us a Saviour who can sympathize with us more strongly, than one who had not been born. But it certainly does give us a Saviour whose sympathy we can better understand. And this is of vast moment. I am not prepared to say that a Superangelic Being, continuing such, might not have entered into all our wants and feelings as truly as one of our race. Our ideas of higher orders of beings are very much perverted, by the habit of comparing them with the higher ranks of men on earth. We are apt to conceive of Angels, as separated from us immeasurably, as filled with the consciousness of their superiority, as looking down upon us with feelings not unlike those with which the aristocracy of this world regard the lower classes of men. The true doctrine, I believe, is, that just in proportion as a being rises in the scale of intelligence and virtue, he becomes knit by tenderer sympathy with inferior orders of being. In truth, he rises above the conception of different orders. He regards all beings, who possess thought, conscience and the power of knowing God, as his Brethren. He respects them as essentially his Equals, in consequence of their capacity of indefinite improvement. He recognizes his own nature in the lowest human creature; and is most solicitous to raise the most fallen. Yes! My belief is, that the beings who sympathize most with human infirmity and sorrow, and who feel most deeply for human guilt, are the beings who are *above* us.

I do not say, then, that Jesus, if he was a Superangelic Being, needed to become a man, in order that he might feel with men. But it was necessary that he should do so, in order that men might trust in his sympathy, and might approach him in fraternal and friendly relations. A being immeasurably raised above us, wearing another form, a stranger to our wants, and clad in celestial splendours, had he come into the world, would have awed and dazzled, but would not have drawn men to free, familiar and affectionate intercourse. Before such unwonted grandeur, the human mind would have sunk, under the consciousness of inferiority. Its faculties would have been fettered, and its free agency checked. Such a heavenly stranger would have been unintelligible. The language of human affection, coming from his lips, could not have been literally interpreted. The multitude would not have understood how, within such a form, dwelt a Brother's heart, and the sensibility of one "born of woman." It was an inestimable advantage, derived from the human birth of Jesus, from his being subjected to all human wants and trials, from his sustaining our natural relations, that his human emotions, his sympathies, his feeling of universal brotherhood, found free and constant scope for manifestation, and that the reality of this bond was felt.

I should say that the greater the Redeemer, the stronger was the necessity of his veiling his greatness and of his appearing in the form of a man, and of the lowliest man. Nothing was so needful, as that the Saviour of men should be comprehended in his Virtues and in his Precepts. And for this end, it was important that he should be divested of everything that might overpower the senses; and that men should be encouraged to approach him nearly, to watch and read his mind in his countenance, tones and movements, and to make him the object of their deliberate scrutiny. To this end, I conceive, the miracles of Jesus were studiously performed in the most unostentatious way. He seemed anxious to veil his majesty under the love with which they were wrought. Stupendous works, which would have overwhelmed the human mind, would have pre-

vented all comprehension of the true character of
Jesus. Accordingly, whilst his miracles had an
inherent grandeur, and were performed with a simple dignity, that proved his Divine Mission, they
were so tempered with mildness and beneficence as
to leave the spectator in the use of his faculties,
and to reveal Jesus as the Friend and ˉBrother as
well as Lord of the human race.

These views should teach us how much we owe
to the human birth of Jesus. That placed him in
the midst of us. That made him one of ourselves.
We can now understand him. We can confide in
his sympathy. I feel, indeed, as if, with my present
views of the heavenly world, I should not shrink before an archangel. But these views I owe to Christianity. They were unknown when Jesus appeared.
And perhaps I deceive myself. Perhaps with an
archangel's form, I could not associate the idea of
fraternal sympathy. But with Jesus, who was born
at Bethlehem, I can form this association. He wore
our Nature; and therefore I know that our Nature
is honoured by him, and is precious to him. He
was born of woman, thus becoming the Brother of us
all; and I therefore know that he feels a Brother's
love for all. I am, indeed, profoundly impressed
with his greatness. I know no superior greatness
save that of the Infinite Father. But his human
birth, and his participation of human nature, make
that greatness endearing and encouraging, not over-

whelming and exclusive. Great as he is, he was still born of a woman. That head was pillowed on a mother's breast. Those eyes shed tears over human sorrow. He had sensibility to pain, as we all have, and shrank with natural horror from an agonizing death. Thus he was one of us. He was a Man. I see in him a Brother and a Friend. I feel the reality of that large, loving, *human* sympathy, which so gloriously distinguished his whole Character and Life. Let us rejoice then that Christ the Saviour was *born*.

II.—In the next place let us rejoice that the birth of Jesus was so *humble*. He was cradled in a manger! I repair to that lowly spot, and look on that infant born in poverty, with a complacency which no condition, however splendid, would give me. And I thus feel great joy, because the humble birth of Jesus was an introduction to the hardships and sufferings of his career. His manger was the foreshadow of his cross. And to the sufferings and the cross of Jesus, more than to all else, do we owe our knowledge of his Spirit, Mind, and Character; of the peculiar strength, tenderness, disinterestedness and expansiveness of his sympathy and love.

To this view I ask your attention. I rejoice then in the clouds which gathered early, and continually thickened around the outward lot of Jesus, because the light within him broke through and

changed them into resplendent glory. Our great
privilege as Christians is that we know the MIND
and the CHARACTER of Jesus, and these were
brought out by the condition in which he was
placed. How often great virtue is hidden, how
often great power slumbers, for want of an appropriate sphere, for want of the trials, by
which alone true greatness can be revealed. Had
Jesus been born under a regal roof, rocked in
the cradle of ease, and surrounded from birth
with imposing pomp, he might have lavished gifts
with a bountiful hand, but the omnipotence of his
love would never have been known as it now is.
He would have encountered no opposition; and
therefore his chief victories—the victories of his
calm courage, of his unconquerable philanthropy—
could not have been won. How entirely he gave
himself up to the work of love we should not have
conceived. Jesus on a throne, followed at every
step by obsequious multitudes, hearing no sounds
but shouts of praise, anticipated in every want,
obeyed at the slightest intimation of his will, might
have loved us as earnestly as did the poor and
persecuted Jesus; but who could have looked into
the depths of his Soul? Who could have measured
the energy of his Goodness? Who would have
comprehended that a Mind of a *new order* had
come to act on human affairs? When is it, that
I learn to know and feel the Mind of Jesus? It

is when I see him associating with the ignorant and lowly, and conforming himself to their lot, that he might more effectually bring great truths within the reach of their intelligence, and might enrich them with new virtues and hopes. It is when I see him beset with foes, spies and slanderers, meeting, wherever he looks, the malignant eye, the dark frown, the whispered taunt, the insulting sneer, and yet giving out the treasures of Divine Truth, with unaltered constancy and meekness. It is when I see him betrayed into the hands of murderers, and recompensed for his blameless and beneficent life by death in its most humbling and dreaded form, and yet holding fast the cause of mankind which God had entrusted to him, and returning their curses with prayers for their forgiveness. At such seasons, I approach the Mind of Jesus. I understand him. And so much do I prize this knowledge, that I rejoice in the humble birth through which he was enabled thus to manifest himself.

To this comprehension of the Mind and Character of Jesus Christ, I attach infinite importance. To me, it is the greatest good received from him. In so saying, I know that I differ from many Christians, who rejoice in Christ's birth chiefly because he came, as they think, to purchase, by his sufferings, the pardon of their sins. I rejoice in his birth, chiefly because he came to reveal, by his suffering, his Celestial Love,—to lay open to us his Soul, and thus to regenerate the human soul. To regenerate and exalt human souls was Christ's ultimate end. And by what means could he more effectually have ministered to this end, than by manifesting, as he did, his own excellence, disinterestedness and Divine Love? This seems to me more and more to be the great good which we derive from the birth of Jesus. His inmost Spirit was thus laid open to us. Nothing has wrought so powerfully on the human soul, as the Mind and Character of Jesus Christ. Among all means of civilization and improvement, I can find nothing to be compared in energy with this. The great impulse which is to carry forward the human race, is the CHARACTER of Jesus, understood ever more clearly, and ever more deeply felt. And consequently I rejoice in his human and humble birth, because by this his Character was brought out. Thus was he revealed as the express Image of Divine Perfection.

And here I cannot but admire and adore the wisdom of Providence. I see how, by means most unpromising to men's view, the greatest purposes of Heaven may be accomplished. Who of us, on visiting the manger of Bethlehem, and beholding an infant amidst accommodations provided for animals, would not have seen in these circumstances the presage of an obscure lot? And yet this lowly birth was the portal to that glorious though brief career, through which the Greatest Mind established an imperishable sway over Humanity. In that infant the passing spectator saw only the heir of poverty, and pitied his hard fate. And yet before that infant, the brightest names of history have grown dim. The Cæsar, whose decree summoned the parents of Jesus to Bethlehem, is known to millions, only through the record of that infant's life. The sages and heroes of antiquity are receding from us, and history contracts the record of their deeds into a narrow and narrower page. But time has no power over the Name and Deeds and Words of Jesus Christ. From the darkness of the past they shine forth with sunlike splendour. Such affection does his peculiar Character inspire, that to thousands now living, the intervening ages since his advent seem annihilated. They place themselves amidst the crowds who followed him; they hear his voice, they look on his benignant countenance; they cherish intimacy with him, almost as if he were yet on earth. No other fame can be compared with that of Jesus. He has a place in the human heart, that no one who ever lived has in any measure rivalled. No Name is pronounced with a tone of such love and veneration. All other laurels wither before his. His are kept ever fresh with tears of gratitude. And this peculiar glory Jesus owes to the humility in which he was born. For it was in his humble, poor, suffering, persecuted life, that he showed, and could alone have showed, the Spirit which has enshrined his Form in the heart of all ages.

You see, then, why I delight in the human and the humble birth of Jesus. It lays open to me his Character, his Mind, his Spirit, his Divine Goodness. Others are more interested in studying Christianity under different aspects. Not a few attach supreme importance to the right decision of the question, "what Rank Jesus holds in the universe,—whether he be God, Archangel, or Man?" Such inquiries it is nowise my wish to discourage; for all truth has its value. But for myself I ask to comprehend the CHARACTER of Jesus. I ask to approach his pure Spirit, to learn his thoughts, feelings, emotions, principles, purposes. I ask to comprehend more and more of that Love, which was so calm, yet so intense, within his heart. I ask to comprehend that expanded Philanthropy which embraced a world,—that tender Philanthropy which, amidst this unbounded expansion, entered into the griefs and wants of the obscurest individual, — that disinterested Philanthropy which could surrender and endure all things even for the evil and unthankful,—that spiritual Philanthropy, which looked with constant and infinite concern on the Soul of man, which felt for his sins far more than for his pains, which reverenced him as

Immortal, and thirsted to exalt him to Immortal Excellence. These are the *Mysteries* of Theology which I am most anxious to explore. To understand Christ's Rank, I should esteem a privilege;— yet I may know this, and be no better and happier for the truth. But to discern the beauty, loveliness, harmony and grandeur of his Mind, this is a knowledge which cannot but exert a creative and purifying power on every one who can attain to it.

I have spoken, with unusual strength, of the infinite importance of knowing the Mind and Spirit of Jesus; and I have so done, because it seems to me not sufficiently appreciated. To this knowledge I ascribe chiefly the efficacy of the Religion, which Jesus taught, and its happy influence upon society. And if this view can be established, you will agree with me in prizing his Birth, chiefly as the means of making known to us his peculiar Character.

I affirm, then, that the efficacy of the Christian Religion lies chiefly in the Character of Jesus. Christianity, separated from Jesus, wanting the light and comment of his Character, would have done comparatively little for the world. Jesus, with his Celestial Love, is the LIFE of his Religion. The Truths of Christianity, had they come to us as abstract principles, would have been comparatively impotent. I might have received from a common

messenger of God the same Precepts which fell
from Jesus.   But how different are these precepts
in quickening power, when coming from those holy
lips, from that warm and noble heart, from that
Friend who loved me so tenderly, and died that
these Laws of Life might be written on my soul!
The Perfect Charity that Jesus inculcates, if taught
by a Philosopher, would have been a beautiful speculation, and might have hovered before me as a
bright vision.   But could I have that faith in its
reality which I now possess, as I see it living and
embodied in Jesus?   What an all-animating hope
of realizing this virtue in my own person springs
up, now that I see in Jesus an inexhaustible desire to
infuse it into every human heart, and am taught
that this Inspiring Influence was the very purpose
of his life and death!   Other Sages have spoken
to me of God.   But from whom could I have learned
the essence of Divine Perfection, as from him, who
was in a peculiar sense the Son, Representative,
and Image of GOD,—who was especially an Incarna-
tion of the unbounded Love of the FATHER?   And
from what other teacher could I have learned to
approach the Supreme Being with that Filial
Spirit, which forms the happiness of my Fellowship
with Him?   From other Seers I might have heard
of Heaven; but when I behold in Jesus the *Spirit*
of Heaven, dwelling actually upon earth, what a
new comprehension have I of that better world!

And when at last I see him returning, through a life and death of all-enduring devotedness, to those pure Mansions of the Blest, how much nearer are they brought to me! What a new power does Futurity, thus associated with Jesus, exert upon the mind! The Spirit of Jesus is thus the true life-giving energy of his Religion; and well we may rejoice in the human and humble birth, by which his peerless Character was made to shine forth so gloriously before "All People," throughout all ages.

In these remarks I have not uttered speculations. There are many strong facts to show that the Spirit of Love in Jesus, which was brought out and manifested by his humble, suffering lot, has been a fresh spring of human improvement, and has given its chief efficacy to his religion. In truth, for many ages scarcely any element of the Christian Religion was left, except the benevolent Character of Jesus. All else was obscured; and the good influences of Christianity proceeded almost wholly from this source. After the irruption of the Northern Barbarians into the Roman Empire, the Christian Religion suffered a mournful eclipse. The true character of God, as the Father, was in a great degree hidden to view. He was conceived of as a partial and vindictive Sovereign, to be propitiated by outward rites. And a system of theology and of ceremonies, corresponding with this fundamental error, supplanted primitive Christianity. Still the Character of Jesus was not lost. God appeared as a terrible Tyrant. But Jesus on his cross still breathed mercy and peace. The central thought, connected with him, was that of infinite clemency, of boundless sympathy, of a charity that could not fail. The Crucifix, before which the barbarian bowed, was the emblem and witness of *all-suffering love.* And it did appeal to the barbarian's rude heart. It kept alive a spark of humanity in his breast. Hence in the darkest ages hospitals were founded. Amidst the clash of arms, and the fierce vengeance of feudal barons, helpless misery was sacred. It was to the love of Christ, bleeding on his cross, that we owe the noblest institution of the Middle Ages—Chivalry. Chivalry, indeed, borrowed its courage from the spirit of the Age, and the indomitable energy of the North. But its peculiar glory, its dedication to the cause of the weak, the wronged, the unprotected,—this noble element of humanity,—shone out from Christ. And, through this, Chivalry became a blessing to the world. Thus the SPIRIT of Christ, which his human and humble birth brought forth, has been working out man's redemption, in the darkest and most disastrous times of Christendom.

We shall see still more clearly the power of the Spirit of Jesus, if we consider the great distinction between the Modern and the Ancient world. What

constitutes the chief superiority of modern times?
I know there are those who say, we have no superiority. But how any man can read Ancient
history, and not perceive the immense advance of
the Human Race, amazes me. We have not advanced indeed as we should and might have done.
And in some qualities antiquity surpassed us. But
there is one glorious element in the present condition
of Society that fills me with ever-new gratitude and
hope. In the Christian world appears a *Spirit of
Humanity*, utterly unknown in the ancient world.
Man looks upon his fellow-man as he never looked
before. New and sacred ties now bind all men
together. There is at work a Philanthropy,—which
not only descends with sympathy and aid to the
lowest depths of social misery,—but which looks
beyond the bounds of the neighbourhood, and of
the nation, with warm concern for the interests of
the whole Family of Man. This Spirit is a promise
to the world infinitely brighter, than was given by
the highest intellectual culture of antiquity. This
principle is still weak, indeed, even in the most
favoured countries. In our own, it has not yet
been strong enough to make us recognize in the
Negro and the Indian our Brethren, with rights
as sacred, and souls as precious, as our own. Still,
this Spirit of Brotherhood, of Friendship, of Humanity, is at work throughout Christendom, and
thence throughout the world. Whence came this

Spirit? It was cradled in the manger at Bethlehem. It traversed Palestine doing good, healing the sick, comforting the mourner, forgiving the wrong-doer, reconciling the sinful, heralding a reign of Peace and Love. And thence, through ages dark and desolate, it has descended to us. Shall we not rejoice, then, in the human and humble birth of our Brother, Friend and Saviour? How through many centuries has he transformed millions into his own Image, by the charm of his Character and the inspiring power of his Life! How mighty is the sway of His Spirit now! Continually we meet persons who have been drawn to Jesus by his Divine Goodness, and moulded into a kindred virtue. When I behold these exalted forms of human nature; when I recognize how, under the influence of his heavenly disinterestedness, the human soul subdues its self-love, cherishes tender, generous, refined and expansive affections towards all fellow-beings, and rises in filial adoration to fellowship with the Infinite Father;—I feel with peculiar gratitude how much we owe to the lowly birth of our Saviour. For in this nobility of soul, which he already confers, we have an earnest of that Perfection, which he has promised to all his followers. And this Perfect Life is true Salvation.

III.—Thus are we led to ask, in what sense the Babe born in the Manger at Bethlehem became and is a Saviour? The answer is sublime,

as it is simple. Jesus Christ is the Great EMANCI-
PATOR. He came to set the Spirit of Man *free*. He
came to give Liberty to Human Nature, through the
whole range of its affections, faculties and energies,
and throughout the whole scope of its being and
destiny. Thus is he the Saviour. Time permits
but a few illustrations of this grand theme.

1. Jesus came to free the Intellect; to give
man liberty of thought, and break the chains in
which the reason had been held; to inspire an
earnest love of truth, and to animate men in its
pursuit,—unfettered by their own passions, prejudices
and interests, and by the customs, traditions and
authority of others. Christianity is the Charter of
Intellectual Liberty, authorizing and commanding
every man to use freely his own faculties in discovering Truth, and especially Religious Truth. This is
a liberty that Christians have thus far too little
prized, though it lies at the root of all other
liberty, and is indispensable for the development
of the human mind. When we regard the many
forms of oppression yet prevalent in the world, we
find none more mournful than the oppression of
Intellect. Everywhere we see men surrendering
their free thought to the yoke of superstition,
through sloth, fear and self-interest, and hugging
their prejudices of education and training as chains
were never hugged before. Their minds have no
free play. In most countries the man who should

stray beyond the beaten path of belief would meet
at his first step penalty and torture, suspicion
and infamy, to drive him back. We know this
to be true in the vast regions overshadowed by
Heathenism, Mahomedanism and Roman Catholi-
cism. Would that tyranny over the mind stopped
there ! Would that on entering Protestant countries we could feel ourselves breathing a free air!
But the mind wears its chains, though lighter
ones, even here.

But Jesus came to set Thought free for a Divine
Destiny. " Prove all things, hold fast that which
is good," is the eternal precept of his religion.
He asserted and proclaimed the rights of every
rational being, and summoned human Reason to its
great function of deliberate inquiry into the " deep
things of God." The human mind was made for
Truth, not for a few truths, but for unbounded
acquisition of all truth. Its nature is as expansive
as the air we breathe, as radiant as the light that
penetrates and pervades the universe. It was made
to go for ever forward. It delights in new and ever-
wider views of God and His work, of nature and
itself; and under all the chains which it has been
made to wear, it has still struggled and striven after
boundless liberty,—so irrepressible is its innate energy.
What progress it is to make under the increased
freedom which it begins to enjoy, one hardly dares
to conjecture. That it is to gain ever-brighter

light; that it will throw off the gloomy errors of theology, which have shut it in like dungeon walls, for ages, and will embrace a Christianity incomparably purer and nobler than we now hold, I cannot doubt. That Age of Light will understand, as we cannot, what is the worth of the intellectual liberty which Christ came to bestow.

2. Jesus came not only to liberate the Intellect, but to be the Emancipator of the oppressed Conscience; to break the power of the passions; to redeem and seat on the throne of human nature the Moral Power; to give new life and range to the law of Duty; to present a glorious Ideal of goodness and greatness, so that the mind may aspire after a lofty Rectitude, such as worldly morality, drawn from prudence and utility, and seeking chiefly security and comfort, never dreamed of.

We are all conscious, however partially, that in human nature there is a Principle that delights in heroic virtue, that admires and reveres men illustrious for self-sacrificing devotedness, that feeds with joy on fictions wherein fellow-beings, amidst great trials and perils, are faithful to duty, and act with noble disinterestedness, at every cost. We all have experienced, in some degree, the workings of this Superior Nature, so as to rejoice with triumphant sympathy, when we read the memoirs of men and women, refined from self-love, pure in principle, consecrated to grand purposes, ascending by lives of ever-enlarging love to the blessedness of a heavenly world. Now this high power of heart and will, that prompts us to aspire after Perfect Excellence, Jesus came to set free. His aim was to enlarge and invigorate it, to exalt it to supremacy, and by his own character, example and influence, to win and welcome it to that Divine Goodness, which it impels us to pursue.

3. Again, Jesus came not only to emancipate the Intellect and Moral Power, but to set free our imprisoned Energy of Love. Man was made for love; he lives by love; and the measure of his life is the largeness and liberty of his love. He is born into the arms and nourished on the breast of love. And in domestic life we often see developed an almost miraculous force of disinterested affection. But the Human Heart was not designed to be confined to home, however heavenly that home may be. Its emotions naturally flow outward, circle beyond circle, in ever-widening waves of sympathy, embracing in their compass a constantly enlarging sphere, and blending at length with the commingling currents and tides of love of the whole Race. But there are antagonistic elements also in human nature, which tend to immure the Individual within himself, and to make him the slave of his selfishness. Now it is the glorious characteristic of Christ's salvation, that it sets at liberty our Love, breaks down the prison walls of self, and carries us freely forth

into this goodly universe,—as the Home of our Father and of His vast Family; that it instructs us how to find objects for our largest affections in all God's children; that it encourages us to identify our private welfare with the advancing good of humanity; that it quickens us to interlink ourselves with all mankind of all classes and conditions, —by reverent admiration with the good, by reconciling mercy with the evil, by cheerful sympathy with the happy, by tender compassion with the suffering, by redeeming pity with the oppressed, by hope with all,—and thus to make our own lives entirely one with the life of our Race. There is an exulting joy in this enlargement of Personal Being; and this limitless expansion of Love was an essential aim of our Saviour.

4. But this is not all. Jesus came not only to liberate the Intellect, the Conscience and the Energy of Love. He came to bring a yet nobler Salvation, by delivering the Soul from the enthralling sway of Creation, and lifting it into communion with the Creator. No man knows Human Nature, till he discerns in it that Central Principle, which might well be called the Love of the Infinite. The profoundest, sublimest, grandest emotion in Man is the longing for an Unbounded Good, the aspiration to be One with the All-Good. We grow weary of whatever is limited. For ever and everywhere we overpass all bounds. The Infinite Creator quickens

in the inmost essence of the soul this insatiable
desire, for which He only is the sufficing Object,
which He alone by His own overflowing Fulness can
gratify. The diverse and multiplied forms of Good
in Creation may for a time bewilder, oppress and
imprison this Divine Principle ; but they cannot
destroy it. For ever it awaits the deliverer. Now
Jesus came to set this Love of the Perfect free. The
true redemption opens, when the Soul, long captive
to the visible, the tangible, the material, resumes
its sovereignty,—and begins to ascend to its Heavenly Parent, by using the very creatures, which
had enthralled it, as the ministers of its return to
God. What liberty does that Spirit gain, which,
breaking away from all illusions of inferior good,
gives itself freely up in veneration, confidence
and grateful joy to the Infinite Father, in whose
Perfect Character, Purposes and Works, it finds
an everlasting range for its noblest faculties, an
ever-unfolding Object for its loftiest love.

5. There is time but to add in a word, finally,
that Jesus came also to set free the indomitable
principle of Hope, which soars for ever forward, on
unresting pinions, out of each human heart. To
all the unexplored future opens vistas, where fairest
prospects bloom and unfading joys bid welcome.
But hope, if confined to this world, feels itself a
prisoner. Its flights stop suddenly at the grave.
And the impenetrable back-ground, that arrests it,

is an awful gloom. Now Jesus came to dispel that darkness, and to unveil before Hope interminable regions of ever-brightening splendour. What a Salvation, priceless beyond conception, is it, to be delivered from all fear of death; to be at liberty to expatiate through endless ages in expectant Hope; to be assured that our highest attainments here are but the beginning of our everlasting progress; and that there is no height of intelligence, power, beneficence and bliss, to which we are not destined to ascend! Jesus came, he lived, he died, to give to us the Universe, and the God of the Universe, by bringing our Spirits into harmony with both,— by breathing into us, so far as we are receptive, the Spirit, Wisdom, Love and Holiness, the Perfect Joy and Peace, of our Heavenly Father. Receive, honour, follow, love this blessed Saviour! Carry into life his principles. Confide in his promises, till they transform you into the Divine Image, and give you in this world the pledge and foretaste of the world to come.

Compassionate Saviour! We welcome thee to our world. We welcome thee to our hearts. We bless thee for the Divine Goodness thou hast brought from Heaven; for the Souls thou hast warmed with love to man, and lifted up in love to God; for the efforts of Divine Philanthropy which thou hast inspired; and for that hope of a pure Celestial Life, through which thy disciples triumph over death.

Benevolent Saviour! Inspirer of Goodness! We offer thee this tribute of affectionate and reverential gratitude on earth; and we hope to know, to love, to resemble and to approach thee, more nearly and more worthily in Heaven.

X.

THE ESSENCE OF
THE CHRISTIAN RELIGION.

THE ESSENCE OF
THE CHRISTIAN RELIGION.

The Glorious Gospel of the Blessed God.—1 Tim. i. 11.

THESE words express the excellence of the Christian Religion. It is called the Gospel, that is, Good News. It is called the Glorious Gospel of the Blessed God, to denote the magnificence of the truths and blessings which it reveals. In this discourse I propose to set before you what it is in Christianity that gives it the chief claim to this high praise. I wish to exhibit to you its Essential Character, and to show what constitutes it worthy of all acceptation.

I.—I begin with asking, What IS Christianity? In answer to this question, it is not necessary that I should repeat the whole New Testament. This book contains the religion; but every verse is not a separate disconnected truth, so that each must be recited to give you an understanding of Christianity. There is a Unity in the religion of Jesus. And this may be summed up in narrow compass. Through the various Precepts of the New

Testament you can trace One Spirit, of which they are all the forms. Its various Doctrines may be reduced to a few great Truths, perhaps to One Single Truth. Now to understand Christianity, the true method is to extract this ESSENCE, as it were, of the various teachings of our Lord; to rise to this Universal Spirit which pervades all his commands; to seize on this great Central Truth, around which all others gather, and from which all derive their glory. To understand Christianity, is not to view in succession every separate truth and precept, but to understand the relation of these various teachings to one another, and to the Great End in which they all meet;—just as to understand the human body, it is not enough to see the limbs singly and severed from each other, but to observe them in their combination, harmonious order and joint symmetry, as pervaded by one life, and all co-working to fulfil one destiny.

I believe that Christianity has ONE GREAT PRINCIPLE, which is *central,* around which all its truths gather, and which constitutes it the Glorious Gospel of the Blessed God. I believe that no Truth is so worthy of acceptation and so quickening as this. In proportion as we penetrate into it, and are penetrated by it, we comprehend our religion, and attain to a living faith. This great Principle can be briefly expressed. It is the doctrine, that " God purposes, in His unbounded Fatherly Love, to PERFECT THE HUMAN SOUL; to purify it from all sin; to create it after His own image; to fill it with His own spirit; to unfold it for ever; to raise it to Life and Immortality in Heaven:—that is, to communicate to it from Himself a Life of Celestial Power, Virtue and Joy." The elevation of men above the imperfections, temptations, sins, sufferings, of the present state, to a diviner being,—this is the great purpose of God, revealed and accomplished by Jesus Christ; this it is that constitutes the Religion of Jesus Christ—Glad Tidings to All People: for it is a Religion suited to fulfil the wants of every human being.

In the New Testament I learn that God regards the Human Soul with unutterable interest and love; that in an important sense it bears the impress of His own Infinity, its powers being Germs, which may expand without limit or end; that He loves it, even when fallen, and desires its restoration; that He has sent His Son to redeem and cleanse it from all iniquity; that He for ever seeks to communicate to it a Divine Virtue which shall spring up, by perennial bloom and fruitfulness, into Everlasting Life. In the New Testament I learn that what God wills is our PERFECTION; by which I understand the freest exercise and perpetual development of our highest powers—strength and brightness of intellect, unconquerable energy of moral principle, pure and fervent desire for truth, unbounded

love of goodness and greatness, benevolence free
from every selfish taint, the perpetual consciousness
of God and of His immediate Presence, co-operation
and friendship with all enlightenèd and disinterested
spirits, and radiant glory of benign will and beneficent influence, of which we have an emblem—a
faint emblem only—in the Sun that illuminates and
warms so many worlds. Christianity reveals to me
this Moral Perfection of man, as the great purpose
of God.

When I look into man's Nature, I see that Moral
Perfection is his only true and enduring Good; and
consequently the promise of this must be the highest
truth which any religion can contain. The loftiest
endowment of our nature is the Moral Power—
the power of perceiving and practising Virtue, of
discerning and seeking Goodness. Having this as
our essential Principle, we can have but one happiness as our End. There is a guide to felicity fixed
by God in the very *Centre* of our being, and no
other can take its place. Whoever obeys faithfully
this principle of Duty has peace with himself and
with all beings. Whoever silences or withstands
this is at war with himself and with all. And no
hostility can be compared with this. It is not brute
matter with which he is at war. He makes the
Principle of Right in his heart, and in all other
beings, that is, the Highest Principle in the Universe, his reprover and foe. He must reconcile this

Sovereign Power, and must make it his Friend, or despair of happiness. To such a being as this, there is no sufficient good but Moral Perfection. If God do not purpose to raise man to this; if man may not look for this to the mercy, power and inspiration of the Almighty; then he has nothing to hope for worthy the name of Happiness. Christianity is God's best gift, in so far as it proffers to us this only felicity, and places it within our reach; as it reveals this to be the great End of our creation. When Christianity is thus viewed, I understand why its revelations are called "unsearchable riches," and why it is said to express "a love which passeth knowledge."

By this language I do not mean to claim for Christianity the exclusive honour of discovering to us God's purpose of perfecting the human soul. The Soul itself—in its powers and affections, in its unquenchable thirst and aspiration for unattained good—gives signs of a Nature made for an interminable progress, such as cannot be now conceived. When, too, I contemplate the immensity and wonderful order of the Material Creation, and the beautiful structure of its minutest parts, I feel sure that Mind, the yet nobler work of God, must be destined to a more enlarged and harmonious existence than I now experience or behold. Above all, Conscience, in its secret monitions, its promises and forebodings, teaches that there is a futurity for men, where more is to be gained and more endured than is possible or imaginable on earth. But I need a more direct, immediate, explicit testimony to the purpose of God. And such a witness is Christianity. This Religion is not a deduction of Philosophy, resting on obscure truths, and intelligible but to a few. It is a solemn Annunciation from Heaven of human immortality, and of a diviner life than this. And it is sealed by miracles, that is, by Divine Interpositions, which are equally intelligible, striking and affecting to all. I maintain that miracles are most appropriate proofs of a Religion which announces the elevation of man to Spiritual Perfection. For what are miracles? They are the acts and manifestations of a Spiritual Power in the universe, superior to the powers and laws of Matter. And on the existence of such a Power, the triumph of our own Spiritual Nature over death and material influences must depend.

The miracles of Christianity, so far from shocking me, approve themselves at once to my intellect and my heart. They seem to me among the most reasonable as well as important events in human history. I prize them, not because they satisfy the passion for the wonderful,—though this principle is one of the noble indications of our nature. But I prize them as discovering, in a way which all can comprehend, that there is some Real Being mightier than Nature; that there is a Mind which *can*, if it

WILL, suspend or reverse the regular operations of the Material World; that, of consequence, the power of death is not supreme, and that the Mind may ascend to a Perfection which nature cannot give. Christianity, in its miracles and doctrines, is the very charter and pledge which I need of this elevation of the Human Soul. And on this account I recognize it as the Glorious Gospel of the Blessed God, or as a Religion making sure to its sincere disciples the most magnificent good which even Omnipotence can bestow.

I wish, my hearers, that I had power to give you some new conviction of the greatness of this good. How much to be deplored is it, that to so many men, the Perfection of their nature never rises to view as a happiness which may be realized; that the consciousness of the capacity of reaching it, of being made for it, is well nigh stifled. The doctrine of that higher state of their powers and affections, of that purer life which Christianity sets before them, is assented to by vast multitudes with no thorough persuasion. And yet without this persuasion we know nothing of the purpose of our being. A darkness, thicker than night, without a star, hangs over our minds. We know neither ourselves nor our fellow-men. We have no explanation of life, of our sufferings, or of our enjoyments. We want that truth, which gives worth and grandeur to our whole existence; which alone inspires perfect trust in God; which alone teaches us respect for man; which is more than equal to the pressure of all trial; and which can carry us forward against the strength of passion, temptation and all forms of evil. How can this truth, without which we are so poor, be called into energetic life, and become a bright reality to us? It must become so, through our own resolute grasp—by effort, by reflection, by prayer, by resistance of the body, the senses and the outward world, by descending into our own minds, by listening to experience, as it daily teaches that there is no true good which has not its spring in the improvement of our Highest Nature.

II.—The more I think of this Central Truth of Christianity, that is, of God's purpose to raise the Soul to its PERFECTION,—the more I feel the glory and excellence of this Religion; the more I feel that, if it promised other goods, or promised happiness in other forms, it would cease to be glorious. No other Heaven, than that which is found in our own Perfection, would be a good worth living for. This truth I have often insisted on; but it seems to me so transcendent in worth as to merit frequent and earnest inculcation. On the understanding of it, our estimate of Christianity must entirely rest. Lay it down then as a Primary, Fundamental Truth, that to a Moral Being there is but one essential enduring Good—and that is, the health, power and purity of his own Soul. Hold this doctrine intelligently, and you hold the key that is gradually to unlock to you the mysteries of Nature and Providence,—of duty, temptation and happiness,—of this life and the life to come.

This doctrine, that Perfection of Mind is our only happiness, by no means interferes with the great truth that God is our Supreme Good. God is indeed our Eternal Source of happiness. But how? Not by pouring profusely upon us gratifications which we may receive in a passive and inert condition, but by awakening our minds and hearts to action, that we may comprehend His Character and thus derive from Him more and more of His own Perfections. To enjoy God, we must bring Him near to ourselves, by concentrating the strength of our intellect in thought and meditation upon His Goodness and Perfections; and still more must His Perfections be received into ourselves by esteem, veneration, sympathy and the adoption of His Pure Will as our own. I can enjoy God only so far as I receive the Divine Mind into my own. His wise and benevolent purposes must become mine own. I must inhale, if I may so speak, the SPIRIT, that breathes through His Works and His Word. I must approve and choose Rectitude, as He chooses it; that is, love and cleave to it for its own sake. It is only by this diffusion of Himself through my Spiritual Nature, by the elevation which His Perfect Character imparts to my own, that God becomes to me the Enduring and the Highest Good.

The desire which I have to impress this great Truth—that Perfection of the Soul is the only spring of happiness, and consequently that Christianity in revealing this as God's purpose is a glorious religion—induces me to offer a proof or illustration, which I hope will not be thought too refined for a popular address. It is a plain fact, then, that to a being endued with Mind, or to an intelligent Spiritual Being, the highest objects of enjoyment are Other Minds or Other Spiritual Beings. I find pleasure in the knowledge and use of matter and of inferior animals. But they cannot satisfy me. I long for intercourse with beings who partake my own highest nature. And what is it in these Spiritual Beings which is fitted to give me the purest and most enduring delight? I answer: their Moral Excellence. Eclipse this Excellence in the Supreme Being; put out the light of His Wisdom, Rectitude and Omnipotent Goodness; rob fellow-beings of virtuous principle and the capacity of spiritual progress: and *what* would remain in Heaven or on earth to attract and move us, to call forth attachment and trust, to inspire hope and joy? The glory of the Universe would be quenched. This Excellence of Goodness is the one great Object to be enjoyed, on earth or in heaven. There is nothing else which can give enduring gratification. And how, I would ask, is this to be enjoyed, but by a corresponding Excellence in our own spirits? To want this is to want the *organ* by which to discern it in others. Who can fail to recognize, that by degrading his own character, he cuts himself off from the enjoyment of pure and lofty souls; that the practice of vice must seal his eyes to the beauty of virtue; that in narrowing his intellect and heart, he unfits himself for communion with great thoughts and noble purposes in others; and on the other hand, that in proportion as he makes progress towards Perfection, he strengthens the holy and happy bonds which unite him with God and all Excellent Beings, and gains new power to enjoy their excellence?

Mind is the great object to be enjoyed; and this is true to a greater extent than we imagine. Even outward, material Nature derives its chief power of contributing to our happiness, by being a manifestation of Mental or Spiritual Excellence. No one truly enjoys the Creation, but he who sees it everywhere as radiant with *Mind*, and as for ever showing forth the Perfection of its Author. We think, perhaps, that Nature has a beauty of its own, in which we can delight, without reference to any Reality above it. But natural beauty is an image or emblem of harmonious qualities of the Mind. It is a Type of Spiritual Beauty. And

he, to whom the last is not known by consciousness, by the dawning of beauty in his own Soul,
can know and feel but little of the former. Thus
the Perfection of our own minds makes us the heirs
of all good, whether in the Outward or the Spiritual
Worlds. Let us, then, look to no other happiness.
Let us feel that Christianity in revealing this, as
God's purpose towards us, meets all our wants,
and is the most glorious of God's provisions for
His human family.

In this discourse I am aiming to set before you
what I believe to be the Central Vital Principle
of Christianity. I conceive that we understand
our Religion, only so far as this great Principle
becomes pre-eminent to our view, and is seen to
pervade and bind together the whole System. I
have said that all the Doctrines and Precepts of
the Gospel meet in this essential and all-comprehending Truth. The purpose of God to raise
the Soul from the power of moral evil to Perfection—this is the beginning and end of Christianity.
To this all its teachings may be traced up ; into
this all may be resolved. Were there time, I might
survey separately the particular Doctrines of the
Gospel, and show that they all may be referred to
this. I shall now offer, however, one brief illustration only ; but it is an all-sufficing one.

The first great Doctrine of Christianity is the
Parental Character of God. To us there is "One

God even the Father." Christianity has no Truth
to teach more encouraging and inspiring than this.
But what do we mean when we call God our
FATHER. Does this term imply nothing more than
that He created us? He created the stone: is He
therefore its Father? Do we mean that He gives
us bodies and the pleasures of sensitive existence?
These He gives to the bird and insect; but the
Scriptures nowhere call Him their Parent. No!
It is clear that this word expresses a spiritual rela-
tion. It declares God's connexion with the Human
Soul. God is the Father of those beings, and of
those only, whom He has created in His own image,
whom He has gifted with a Spirit like His own, whom
He has framed for the end that they may approach
Him in His highest attributes. To be a Parent is
to communicate a *kindred nature,* and to watch over,
educate and guide this nature to perfect development.
God loves us as a Father, by loving supremely the
Soul in each of us, and by His intense concern
to conform this Soul to Himself. When you call
God "Father," do not think of him as a fond
indulgent being, anxious only for your enjoyment
here and hereafter. This would be to degrade our
Divine Benefactor. Think of this Father as looking upon the Spirit within you, with unutterable
interest; as desiring for you no happiness but that
of pure Goodness; as purposing your Perfection as
His chief and crowning end in your creation. This

is the only true view of God as our Father. And
thus the doctrine of His Parental Character is one
and the same with the great principle of communicating Moral Perfection, which I have so earnestly
affirmed to be the essence and centre of Christianity.

III.—My friends, the great purpose of God
towards mankind, which I have this day set forth
as the substance of Christianity, is one with which
we cannot be too deeply impressed. We cannot too
thoroughly understand and feel that the Perfection
of our nature, for which God made and redeemed
us, is the highest good and the only true good.
I consider the mind sound, wise, equal to its own
happiness, only so far as it is possessed by this
great truth. To expect happiness by any other
process, than by co-operation with this purpose of
God, is to insure disappointment, and to throw
away our labour and our lives. All other purposes
and all other means of felicity must come to naught.
This great principle we cannot carry out too far.
We may lay it down as universally and unerringly
true, that nothing contributes to the enduring happiness of Individuals, or of Communities, but what
contributes to this PERFECTION of Human Nature.
Individuals and Communities are perpetually seeking good in other ways, but only to reach disastrous
failure and shame.

At this period, we see a mighty movement of

the civilized world. Thrones are tottering, and the firmest establishments of former ages seem about to be swept away by the torrent of Revolution.[*] In this movement I rejoice, though not without trembling joy. But I rejoice, only because I look at it in the light of the great Truth which I have this day aimed to enforce; because I see, as I think, in the Revolutionary Spirit of our times, the promise of a freer and higher action of the Human Mind,—the pledge of a State of Society more fit to perfect human beings. I regard the present state of the world in this moral light altogether. The Despotisms, which are to be prostrated, seem to be evils, chiefly as they have enslaved men's faculties, as they have bowed and weighed down the Soul. The Liberty, after which men aspire, is to prove a good only so far as it shall give force and enlargement to the Mind; only so far as it shall conspire with Christianity in advancing Human Nature. Men will gain little by escaping outward despotism, if the Soul continues enthralled. Men must be subjected to some law; and unless the law in their own breast, the Law of God, of Duty, of Perfection, be adopted by their free choice as the Supreme Rule, they will fall under the tyranny of selfish passion, which will bow their necks for an outward yoke.

I have hope in the present struggle of the world,

[*] The Winter of 1830—31.

because it seems to me more spiritual, more moral, in its origin and tendencies, than any which have preceded it. It differs much from the revolts of former times, when an oppressed populace or peasantry broke forth into frantic opposition to government, under the goading pressure of famine and misery. Men are now moved, not merely by physical wants and suff鐤rings, but by Ideas, by Principles, by the conception of a BETTER STATE OF SOCIETY, under which the Rights of Human Nature will be recognized, and greater justice be done to the mind in all classes of the community. There is then an element, —spiritual, moral, and tending towards Perfection,— in the present movement; and this is my great hope. When I see, however, the tremendous strength of unsubdued passions, which mix with and often overpower this conception of a Better Order of Society; when I consider the success with which the selfish, crafty and ambitious have turned to their own purposes the generous enthusiasm of the People; when I consider the darkness which hangs over the Nations, the rashness with which they have rushed into Infidelity and Irreligion, as the only refuge from priestcraft and superstition; and when I consider how hard it is for men, in seasons of tumult and feverish excitement, to listen to the mild voice of wisdom teaching that Moral Perfection alone constitutes glory and happiness;—I fear. I fear not for the final results; not for the *ultimate* triumphs of Truth, Right, Virtue, Piety; not for the gradual melioration of men's lot: but for those nearer results, those immediate effects, which the men of this generation are to witness and to feel.

In such a state of the world, it seems to me of singular importance, that Christianity should be recognized and presented in its true character, as I have aimed to place it before you this day. The low views of our religion, which have prevailed too long, should give place to this highest one. They suited perhaps darker ages. But they have done their work, and should pass away. Christianity should now be disincumbered and set free from the unintelligible and irrational Doctrines, and the uncouth and idolatrous Forms and Ceremonies, which terror, superstition, vanity, priestcraft and ambition have laboured to identify with it. It should come forth from the darkness and corruption of the past in its own celestial splendour, and in its divine simplicity. It should be comprehended as having but one purpose, the Perfection of Human Nature, the elevation of men into nobler beings. I would have it so luminously displayed, that men should distinctly see how it tends, by all its influences and teachings, to the true Freedom of the State, and to the honour and everlasting progress of the Individual. Let Christianity be thus taught and viewed, and it will act as a New Power on human affairs. And unless thus viewed, I despair of its triumphs. The time has gone by in which any Religion is to take a strong and enduring hold on the world, except by offering itself in the high character ascribed to Christianity in this discourse. Men will yield their faith to no system, which does not bear the plain marks of being adapted to the highest principles and powers of Human Nature, and which does not open to it a career of *Endless Improvement*. They are outgrowing unintelligible notions. They understand that the glory of a Religion is to be measured by the moral glory, power, perfection, which it communicates to the Mind. I know not, therefore, how a greater service can be rendered to Christianity, or how its power can be more extended, than by teaching it as a revelation of God's great purpose to perfect His human offspring, and as the great power or instrument by which this Perfection is to be achieved.

My friends, I have been applying our subject to the actual state of the Christian and civilized world. Let me come nearer home. You have heard of God's purpose to purify and perfect the human soul, that He has sent His Son to redeem it from all evil, and to present it spotless before its Creator and Judge. Do you believe this? Have you faith in the Human Soul as formed for a higher life than it can now enjoy? Have you faith in your own Souls, as capable of ascending to sinless purity? Has the

Perfection of your being risen before you as the one glorious good, for which existence was granted, for which its mingled joys and trials were measured out, for which the Father sent His Son from heaven? Do you believe that the blessedness of angels may be yours, and that to this bliss you are welcomed? You believe in God. But how? As the Author of this Outward Universe? This is to pause at the threshold. Do you believe in Him yet more as the Author of an Inner Universe, whose beauty, grandeur, harmony and exceeding excellence transcend immeasurably all that Nature manifests of His Infinite Good-will? You speak of His love. Do you feel that this love is too lofty, too limitless, to content itself with any good that falls short of elevating His Children into companionship with Himself? Have you learned to look through the body to the Immortal Spirit, and to feel that this is infinitely precious to ,the Father of Spirits, and that it should be equally dear to you His Child? This, and this alone, is Christian Faith. Are we wanting in this faith in the destiny of the Soul for Perfection? Then we know Christianity only in the letter, and as a sound. Then the significance of the Glorious Gospel has never brightened on our view. Then the Light of Life has never risen within. Then our own Souls are yet to be revealed to us. Then the all-illuminating Truth, that gives unutterable interest to this infant stage of our existence, has never dawned on us. Then the Eternal Day, with its splendours of consolation, hope, peace and exhaustless power, has not beamed on us in blessing. But this Truth may shine out, if our minds turn towards it. This Day may dawn, and the Infinite Love of Our Father for us rise like the morning. Let us aspire towards this living confidence, that it is the will of God to unfold and exalt without end the Spirit that entrusts itself to Him in well-doing as to a Faithful Creator. And may the "God of all grace, who hath called us unto His eternal glory by Christ Jesus, after that ye have suffered awhile, make you perfect, stablish, strengthen, settle you. To Him be glory and dominion, for ever. Amen."

XI.

PERFECT LIFE

THE END OF CHRISTIANITY.

PERFECT LIFE
THE END OF CHRISTIANITY.

Not every one that saith unto me, Lord, Lord, shall enter into the kingdom of heaven; but he that doeth the will of my Father which is in heaven.—MATTHEW vii. 21.

IN these words we have a light to guide us through the intricate paths and imprisoning walls, which perverse ingenuity has reared around the Temple of God in Man. Here we learn what is central in religion. Here is revealed the immortal good, that Jesus, in his life and death, proposed as his Great End.

To do God's Will,—Duty—Moral and Religious Integrity—Rectitude in principle and practice—the Love of the Father and of all His intelligent offspring in truth and in deed,—this holds the supreme place of dignity, alike on earth and in heaven. Just in so far as we attain to this, we enter even now the Kingdom of Heaven. Would that this Truth might emerge in full glory, out of the obscurity, with which false systems of Theology have enveloped it; that it might break through the clouds of mystery, which have so long shrouded it, and shine with sunlike splendour on our souls. Never can God's Will be *done* with our whole energy, until we learn that there is nothing in time, nothing in eternity, to be compared with the Perfect Life.

I.—By the WILL of God we understand generally His Commands. In the text, Jesus intended particularly the *Precepts* which he was just giving from the Mount; for these words concentrate the Spirit of that memorable discourse. The great truth, to which we are led by this passage, and by the whole New Testament, may be expressed in a few words. I affirm, and would maintain, that *Excellence* of CHARACTER—that the religious, social, self-controlling Virtue, which is set forth in these Precepts, and which pervades the whole teaching of Jesus— is the Great Object of Christianity, is the Great Blessing which Christ came to communicate. I affirm that the highest good which he effects, is that which he works within. His influence on human character is his holiest influence. I insist on this truth,—because, simple as it appears to be, it is not sufficiently understood. The common doctrine is, that Christ came to confer other benefits, and especially to reconcile the offended Deity to His sinful creatures, to shield men from Divine anger and from outward punishment. I believe, on the contrary, that his Great End is to work a change within the mind, spirit, character of

men, and that the glory of this change constitutes the glory of his office. Virtue, rectitude,
purity, love to God, love to man,—in one word,
Goodness,—this is the great good which flows to
us from Jesus Christ. This is the Redemption
he confers. This truth I would now illustrate.

1. That Christ's great purpose is to redeem men
from Sin to Virtue, is the view I meet with perpetually in the SCRIPTURES. I meet it everywhere;
now in direct assertion, now by implication. I
meet it in precept, promise and parable. "His
name shall be called Jesus," says the angel; "for
he shall save his people from their sins,"—that
is, from vice and moral evil. "I came," says Jesus,
"to call men to repentance." "God sent him to
bless us," says Peter, "by turning us from our
iniquities." "He gave himself for us," says Paul,
"that he might redeem us from all iniquity, and
purify unto himself a peculiar people, zealous of
good works." "He died for us, that we, dying
to sin, may live unto righteousness." But it is
unnecessary to multiply quotations. What is plainer
from the whole New Testament, than that reformation, righteousness, the practice of good works,
is the great purpose of our religion, and that whenever this is accomplished, the work of Christianity
is done?

2. I pass from the Scriptures to that Revelation
which always concurs with Scripture,—to REASON;

and I affirm, that from the very nature of God and
of His Universe, Jesus Christ *can* communicate no
greater good than this Virtue,—this Rectitude of
which I have spoken. And I thus affirm, because
this Goodness is the highest good which Jesus himself possesses. We hear much controversy and
contention respecting Jesus Christ. But I ask you:
What was his great distinction? Was it not his
spotless virtue? Place Jesus in what rank you
will, is it not, after all, the *Excellence* of his
CHARACTER,—his disinterestedness—his devotion to
great and good ends—his celestial mildness—his
stainless purity,—which you count the best of all
his endowments? Arm him with power over the
universe, but quench his Charity, and do you not
eclipse his glory? Ascribe to him infinite wisdom,
but pervert the Rectitude of his will, and do you
not even turn such omniscience into a curse alike
to himself and to others? What, I ask, does Jesus
own, so precious, so glorious, as that VIRTUE which
he teaches his disciples? What is it that endears
Jesus Christ to his Father? You may learn it from
the following passage: "Jesus said to his disciples:
If ye keep my commandments, ye shall abide in
my love, even as I have kept my Father's commandments, and abide in His love." I beg you to
weigh these words. Jesus owed the peculiar love,
with which he was regarded by God,—he owed his
office as the Messiah, and all the power with which

he was invested,—to his obedience, to his moral and
religious integrity, to his unfailing reverence for
Goodness. Why was it that he enjoyed such peculiar communion with God? He says: "The Father
hath not left me alone, because I do always those
things which please Him." *This* was the bond
of union between him and his Father. To this
perfect Rectitude of his Will, his Reason and his
Life, he owed not only his mission on earth, but
his crown in Heaven. Paul assures us, that in
recompense of his obedience unto death, he is now
enthroned above all power and dignity, both in this
world and in the world to come. Thus in heaven,
as on earth, Jesus has nothing so precious to bestow
as Goodness. We talk indeed in popular language
of Christ as "sitting on a throne." But how
worthless would be a throne, though made of
heaven's richest treasures, compared with the God-
like Charity that reigns within him and constitutes
his Soul? His real throne is the empire that tried
and triumphant Virtue gives him in that pure realm.
Men talk of the "brightness" which surrounds
him, and of the "splendour of his form"; but
this is only the beaming forth of his Spirit. Mere
outward radiance is dim when compared with his
Intellectual and Moral Perfection. The disputes of
Christians about the Rank of Christ have turned
their minds away from the simple truth taught
throughout in the New Testament,—that his un-

faltering Rectitude,—his undeviating obedience,—
his divine philanthropy,—his perfect accordance
with the Will of his Father,—was, and is, and ever
will be, his supreme glory and his richest joy;
and consequently that he can give nothing more
blessed. In bringing us, by his religion, to *do*
the Will of his Father, he brings us into his own
state of happiness and heaven,—brings us to do
that, in doing which his own blessedness consists,—
brings us into his own kingdom, and shares with
us his own throne. For his Kingdom is but another
name for Righteousness, and his Throne is the sway
that Virtue always wields.

3. I urge this topic, because it seems to me that
no error is more common among all Sects than the
expectation from Christ of some greater good than
Virtue and Holiness,—than a right Spirit towards
God and man. But this includes all good. This
is to the mind what health is to the body, giving
it the enjoyment of all else, bringing it into harmony with God and the Creation, giving it peace
within itself. In an important sense, the spring
of all happiness is in the Mind. True, all happiness is the gift of God. But He gives it through
our own spiritual development, gives it as a fruit
and recompense of growing purity. No happiness
will bloom for us hereafter which has not its germs
in our own rectified minds, which does not spring
from an inward root of wisdom and of love. Future

happiness is not to be a passive good, coming to us from outward sources, a delight which we shall inhale as we now breathe a balmy atmosphere, without a thought or care of our own. Happiness is not to be a stream of pleasure flowing in upon us, whilst we resign ourselves to indolent repose. The happiness of heaven is activity. It is power. It is clear and bright thought, the love of Truth, and the love of Right. It is strengthening friendship and efficient charity. It is consecration of every energy to God—the perception of beauty in all His works—the offering up of gratitude and praise for ever-new and multiplying proofs of His goodness. It is the outflow of our sympathies and attachments, and the communication of nobler blessings to our fellow-creatures. By the happiness of Heaven, I understand the Mind, rising, through acts of piety and virtue, to an enlarged, sublime, creative power of Thought, such as is faintly shadowed forth by the mightiest efforts of Genius upon earth, and to a Pure Love, of which we have dim presages in the most heroic and self-sacrificing deeds of Heroism recorded in history. The happiness of heaven is Moral and Religious Principle, diffused through and perfecting all our faculties, affections and energies; and consequently nothing greater than this Principle of Goodness can be communicated to us by Jesus Christ through everlasting ages. His highest office consists in thus leading us to do the Will of Our

Father in Heaven. In conforming our Minds to the Supreme Mind, he gives us the happiness of heaven; nor can it be given in any other way.

From these remarks you learn that I consider Righteous Action, the DOING OF GOD'S WILL, as the *Beginning and End* of Christianity. I regard the Precepts of Jesus—which he gave on the Mount, and which he illustrated so gloriously in his life —as the Essential Element of his Religion, and to which all other parts are but subservient. Obey these, and the purpose of his religion is fulfilled in you. Regard these as your Rule of Life, and you build your house upon a rock. Live them out in deed, and you have entered the Kingdom of Heaven —you even now enter it. Christ's Precepts then— declaring God's Will, or PERFECT VIRTUE—are what chiefly concern us. To secure obedience to his Precepts is the great aim of all the Doctrines, Promises and other Teachings of Christ. And to exalt these above the Precepts is to prefer the *means* to the END.

II.—1. It may be said, in reply to these views, that whilst I am inclined to lay the whole stress on Obedience and on Perfect Virtue, the New Testament lays the greatest stress on FAITH. "To be saved, we must believe," men say. "Virtue, purity, sanctity, are not enough. Faith in Christ is the possession which is most to be prized." I might reply to this, that Paul taught a different doctrine,

in that memorable passage, where, in comparing
Faith, Hope and Charity, he said, the "greatest of
these is Charity." I waive, however, that reply. I
acknowledge the importance of Faith. But still
I maintain the *supremacy* of virtuous obedience.
For what is Faith, and what is its use? To believe
in Christ is to receive and cherish those great
truths, from which a pure life flows,—by which the
mind is strengthened to withstand evil, to overcome
inward and outward foes, and to press forward to
Perfection. The value of Faith lies in its power
over the character,—in the force of holy purpose,
in the enlargement of philanthropy,—in the union
of the mind to God,—to which it is fitted to exalt
us. In other words, Faith is a *means*, and Obedience
is the END. What is it to believe in Christ? I
answer: It is to believe that he and his religion came
from God, and to follow out in practice this conviction. It is to recognize a divine excellence and
authority in his Precepts, and resolutely to adopt
them as our Rule of Life. It is to see a divine
purity in his Character, and resolutely to make it
our model. It is to be assured that under his
guidance we shall attain to Perfection, and to forsake all other guides for this inestimable good. It is
to believe in the promises which he has made to
all forms of holiness; and under this conviction to
cultivate all. It is to believe that the pure in heart
shall see God; and under this conviction to cleanse

18

the thoughts, imagination and desires. It is to believe that the merciful shall find mercy, and the forgiving be forgiven; and through this confidence to cherish a placable and affectionate virtue. It is to believe the promise, that if we ask we shall receive; and under this persuasion to seek earnestly God's Holy Spirit. In a word, Faith is to believe, that if we hear and do the words which Jesus spake, we shall be like the man, who built his house upon the rock; and in this *confidence* to OBEY. I know nothing plainer than the true use of Faith. It is enjoined wholly for its practical influences, simply to aid and strengthen us to resist sin, and to encourage us to frame ourselves after that PERFECTION of Character which shines forth in the precepts and example of Jesus.

2. Again, it is a common opinion, that LOVE to Christ has some special efficacy, that by this some higher end is accomplished in securing salvation than by a general obedience of his laws. Far be it from me to chill, in the slightest degree, the affection with which Christ is regarded. I feel that he has not yet received from men the love which he deserves. Deeply should I rejoice to set forth with a new power his claims to our reverent esteem and joyful gratitude. But let not this regard to Christ be misunderstood. Especially let it not be separated in our thoughts from obedience to his Precepts, or be exalted in our esteem above general Rectitude.

The truth is, the Love of CHRIST is but another name for the love of VIRTUE. It is not, as some seem to think, a kind of theological emotion—a mysterious fervour—distinct from moral integrity, from philanthropy and from our duties to God and our neighbour. We err grievously if we imagine that our salvation is promoted by occasional ardour towards Christ, which subsists apart by itself, in the heart,—which does not blend with our ordinary feelings and our daily lives. The CHARACTER of Christ *is* PERFECT Virtue. And consequently attachment to Christ, as I have just said, is but another name for attachment to Virtue.

In this consists the excellence of a Love of Jesus, that it is a love of the purest, loveliest, sublimest manifestation of Moral Excellence, and is our surest guide to the attainment of it. To love Jesus Christ is to love him, in whom Human Virtue was revealed in its PERFECTION, and who came that he might communicate to us what was most perfect in his own mind. It is to love disinterestedness, self-sacrifice and an unbounded charity. It is to love a will wholly purified from selfishness, and entirely consecrated to the will and loving purposes of God. It is to love calmness, constancy, fortitude and magnanimity. It is to love a spirit raised above the world, its frowns, its flatteries, its opinions, its prejudices, its most dreaded pains. It is to love him who gave himself for us, that he might rescue us from all sin, and present us spotless to God. Who does not see then that the Love of Christ is one and the same, with a consecration to what is good and great—with the desire of Perfection—with entire devotedness to doing God's Will.

3. I am aware that the importance which I have now attached to the Precepts of Christianity must shock the common prejudice,—that the distinguishing excellence of the Gospel lies in its PECULIAR DOCTRINES. The Doctrines of Christianity I should be the last to undervalue. But I maintain that these Doctrines all bear directly on its Precepts, and are all designed to teach the supreme worth of Christian Virtue. In this all their significance consists. Let me descend to a few particulars.

I am told by some Christians, that the Doctrine of Immortality is the grand discovery of Christianity, and gives it its chief value. But, I ask, why is Immortality revealed? And I answer, it is revealed wholly as a motive to obedience. The Future State, which Jesus Christ brought to light, is a state of Equitable Retribution, where those who do good will rise to glory and honour and peace, and those who do evil to shame, tribulation and anguish. To believe in Immortality is to believe in the everlasting triumph and growth of Virtue; and under this conviction to choose it as our Supreme Good.

Again, some Christians will tell me that the Doctrine of Divine Forgiveness is the great glory of Christianity. But, I ask, to whom is Divine Forgiveness promised? To *all* indiscriminately? Did Christ publish from his Cross absolute, unconditional pardon? Who does not know that throughout the whole teaching of the New Testament, repentance and remission of sins are always combined, and that the last is invariably used as a motive for the first? Who is forgiven in Christianity? The Prodigal! Yes! But not whilst wasting his substance in riotous living; but when, heart-broken, conscience-struck, he returns to his Father's house. Our Father's pardon was promised by Jesus to such as forsake sin, and obey His Will; and this obedience is the End for which Divine Forgiveness is preached.

Again, some Christians may tell me that the Doctrine of Salvation is the great doctrine of Christianity,—more important than all its Precepts, and of more worth than all its incitements to Virtue. Salvation is a sublime doctrine. But what does it mean? According to the Scriptures, salvation is to be rescued from moral evil, from error and sin, from the diseases of the mind, and to be restored to inward truth, piety and virtue. Consequently, Salvation and Christian Obedience are one and the same. Nor indeed can salvation be anything else. I know but one salvation for a sick

man, and that is to give him *health*. So I know
but one salvation for a bad man, and that is to
make him truly, thoroughly, conscientiously *good*,—
to break the chains of his evil habits,—to raise him
to the dignity and peace of a true religious life.
An intelligent and moral being is saved and blessed
just so far as he chooses freely—fully—what is
good, great and god-like; as he adopts for his Rule
the Will of God. I therefore repeat it. Salvation
and Virtue are but different aspects of the same
Supreme Good. But now I go one step further,
and reach the very citadel of controversy.

4. There are Christians, who will tell me, there
is one Principle of the Gospel which constitutes
its very essence, to which I have not even alluded;
and which is of more importance to the human
race than all Christ's Precepts combined. This is
REDEMPTION by the BLOOD of the CROSS. This
Atonement, we are told, is the grand distinction
of the Gospel; and all other parts of Christianity
hold but a subordinate place. "The Cross! the
Cross! is the CENTRE of our Religion," they say,
"round which the Precepts and the Promises re-
volve, and from which all borrow light and life."
To "trust in the Cross" has a more immediate
and important influence on our salvation, than to
carry out in life, however perfectly, all Precepts
of the Sermon on the Mount.

To this I reply, that I prize the Cross and

Blood of Christ as highly as any Christian can. In view of that Cross I desire ever to live; and of that Blood, in the *spiritual sense*, I desire ever to drink. I hope, as truly as any Christian ever did or could, to be saved by the Cross of Christ. But what do I mean by such language? Do I expect that the *wood* to which Christ was nailed is to save me? Do I expect that the *material* blood which trickled from his wounds is to save me? Or do I expect this boon from his bodily agonies? No! By the cross and blood of Christ, I mean nothing outward, nothing material. I mean the Spirit, the Character, the Love of Jesus, which his death made manifest, and which are pre-eminently fitted to bind me to him, and to make me a partaker of his virtues. I mean his Religion, which was sealed by his blood, and the Spirit of which shone forth most gloriously from his cross. I mean the great Principles for which he died, and which have for their sole end to purify human nature.

According to these views, the blood and cross of Christ are the means of Christian Virtue. How then can they be exalted above that Virtue? I am astonished and appalled by the gross manner in which "Christ's Blood" is often spoken of, as if his outward wounds and bodily sufferings could contribute to our salvation; as if aught else than his Spirit, his Truth, could redeem us. On other

occasions we use the very words, which we thus
apply to Christ, and use them rationally. How is
it that in religion we so readily part with our *common sense?* For example, we often say that our
liberty was purchased, and our country was saved,
"by the *blood* of Patriots." And what do we
mean?—that the material blood which gushed
from their bodies, that their wounds, that their
agonies, saved their country? No! We mean that
we owe our freedom to men who loved their country
more than life, and gladly shed their blood in its
defence. By their blood we mean their patriotism,—
their devotion to freedom,—approved in death. We
mean their generous heroism, of which death was
the crown. We mean the Principles for which they
died, the Spirit which shone forth in their self-
sacrifice, and which this sacrifice of their lives
spread abroad and strengthened in the community.
So by Christ's Blood I understand his Spirit, his
entire devotion to the cause of Human Virtue and
to the Will of God. By his Cross I mean his
Celestial Love,—I mean the great Principles of piety
and righteousness,—in asserting which he died. To
be redeemed by his blood is to be redeemed by his
Goodness. In other words, it is to be purified from
all sin, and restored to all virtue, by the principles,
the religion, the character, the all-conquering love
of Jesus Christ. According to these views, Moral
Purity, Christian Virtue, Spiritual Perfection, is the

Supreme Good to be bestowed by the blood and cross of Christ. O! that a voice of power could send this simple yet most sublime Truth to the utmost bounds of Christendom! It is a truth mournfully and disastrously obscured. According to common views, the Death of Christ, instead of being the great *quickener* of heroic virtue, is made a SUBSTITUTE for it; and many hope to be happy through Christ's dying agony, much more than through the participation of his Self-sacrificing Life. I doubt, whether any error has done so much to rob Christianity of its purifying and ennobling power, as these false views of Atonement. The Cross of Jesus—when supposed to bless us by some mysterious agency of reconciling God to us, and not by transforming our characters into the spirit and image of our Saviour—becomes our peril, and may prove our ruin. Of one reality I am SURE, and I speak it with entire confidence. I cannot receive from the Cross of Christ any good so great, as that sublime Spirit of SELF-SACRIFICE, of Love to God, and of unbounded Charity, which the Cross so gloriously manifested. And they who seek not this, but seek, as they imagine, some mystical and mysterious good, from Christ's death, are mournfully blinded to the chief End of Christianity. I speak thus strongly,—not in arrogance, not in uncharitableness,—but because a great Truth, felt deeply, cannot utter itself feebly and tamely; because no language, less emphatic, would be just to the strongest convictions of my conscience, my reason and my heart.

III.—My friends, I have stated in this discourse the Great Good which Jesus Christ came to spread through the earth—the highest benefit which he can confer. I know nothing of equal worth with Moral Excellence; with an enlightened, powerful, disinterested and holy mind; with a love to God which changes us into His likeness. I know nothing so important to us as the PERFECTION of our own Spirits. Perfect Goodness is the SUPREME Good, may I not say *the only good?* We often hear, indeed, of the Rewards of virtue, as if they were something separate from virtue, and virtue was but the means. But I am sure that Virtue itself is worth more than all outward rewards; its truest recompense is found in *itself*, in its own growing vigour, in its own native peace, in the harmony which it establishes between our souls and God, in the sympathy and friendship by which it identifies us with the Universe. So we hear of the Punishments of sin as if they were the greatest evils to be dreaded. But Sin, I am sure, is *itself* more terrible than all its consequences, more terrible than any hell; and its chief misery is bound up in its own hateful nature. Of course, the only redemption of a human being is the recovery of his Spirit from moral evil, from whatever stains and debases it, to the purity, philanthropy, piety and perfectness of a Child of God, such as was manifested in the Beloved Son.

To do the Will of our Heavenly Father,—to form ourselves after the purest Ideal of Goodness, which Nature, Conscience, Revelation present as a pattern,—is the great work of earthly existence. This practical use of the Gospel is the only saving Faith in Jesus Christ. For we know him, and believe in him, only in so far as we recognize, love and imitate the Perfection of his Character and Life. To prefer Universal Rectitude, the boundless Love of God and fellow-beings, the PERFECT LIFE, before all other good, is the only true wisdom, is the only real worship. We know nothing of a Future World, unless we hear proceeding from it a Voice of Benediction, that warns and welcomes us to enter now into that Purity, Integrity, Charity, Holiness, Peace and Joy, which are the bliss of Heaven.

XII.

THE CHURCH UNIVERSAL.

THE CHURCH UNIVERSAL.

There is One Body, and One Spirit, even as ye are called in One Hope of your calling.—EPHESIANS iv. 4.

THIS passage declares the living Unity that will bind all Christians together, in proportion as they are filled with the Spirit of their Religion, and are joined vitally to their common Head. They constitute One Body. Christians are not distinct, separate, independent followers of Christ, each walking in a lonely path, living by an undisclosed faith, locking up in the breast an unparticipated love. Christ came not merely to teach a Doctrine, but to establish a Church, to form a Religious Society, to organize a Spiritual Community. His religion was revealed to be a common possession, a common joy, a common ground of gratitude and praise, of sacrifice and work, for the whole Human Race. His religion was intended to be a world-wide cause, in which innumerable multitudes should be leagued; which should be advanced by their united prayers, aspirations, toils and sufferings; which one age should transmit to another; which should enlist

men of a devout and disinterested spirit through
all nations and times. Christ is not the leader
of solitary Individuals. The titles given to him
in the New Testament imply the most close and
endearing connexions among those whom he calls
his "Friends." Christ is the Head, and Christians
are his Body—living members one of another. He
is the Corner-stone, and they are a Temple—built
on him as a foundation, gaining strength and
proportion from the fit junction of its various materials and parts. He is the Shepherd, and they
are the Flock. Christianity is thus pre-eminently
a Social Religion,—disposing its disciples to joint
services,—awakening the feeling. of brotherhood,—
demanding concerted efforts for its development and
diffusion,—and in a word combining all believers
into organic Unity in Spirit and in Deed.

I.—It might be anticipated that a Religion coming
from man's Creator, whose Essence is LOVE, should
be a Social one. For man, by his very nature, is
pre-eminently a Social Being.

All the great developments of humanity are fulfilled through Society. Society surrounds us at
our entrance into life, and its influences embrace
us till the parting hour. The arms of fellow-
beings receive us at birth, and enfold us at death.
The first and last sounds we hear are human
voices. Thus social ties entwine themselves about
our whole existence from the cradle to the grave.

The happiness experienced in loving and being loved, the enhanced joy which blessings derive from participation, the resources which infancy and age, infirmity and disease, find in the affectionate sympathy, sustenance and strength of the home circle, the pleasures of friendly discourse and the solaces of fraternal confidence, the astonishing enterprises achieved by the union of thoughts and energies in communities and nations, the light of literature, art, science, law, religion, transmitted and brightened by transmission from mind to mind, and from age to age,—countless benefits indeed, which there is no time to enumerate,—attest the benignant purposes of our Heavenly Father in making us Social.

The Influence of Society upon the character of its constituent members can hardly be overstated. At times it even absorbs man's free agency. Individuals are moulded by the community, in which they live, almost passively and unconsciously. What a striking example we have of the power of Society over individual persons in the unfailing transmission of national characteristics from generation to generation! In what ineradicable lines of feature and form, of temperament and tendency, is this influence graven! What multiplied traces in physiognomy, and in intellectual and moral traits, does every man bear of the People, among whom he has chanced to be born! Souls pour

19

themselves imperceptibly, but copiously, into other souls. So swift, subtle and strong is this spiritual commerce between person and person, that a look or a tone is enough to reveal mind to mind, and to change the whole current of one another's thoughts and emotions. Feelings, which sleep within us in solitude, awaken into intense energy, when manifested powerfully by those around us. And a multitude, by acting upon one another, are wrought into fervours either of generous enthusiasm or of indignant passion, to which our nature under ordinary circumstances is wholly unequal.

Again, there is a principle of expansion in the soul, an ardent thirst for great objects and wide spheres of affection and action, which, in all lands and times, manifests itself in magnanimous Patriotism. How this generous love of country overcomes the contracting influences of our present selfish stage of civilization. Every day we see men of no uncommon capacity or elevation of character devoted to the interests of the community in which they, live, proud in its glory, exulting in its triumphs, humbled in its humiliations, wedded to its fortunes, sacrificing all private good for its advancement, clinging to it in peril, hazarding life in its defence. Reproach cast upon their nation stings them more keenly than personal insult. Its most distinguished lawgivers, heroes and men of genius, though belonging to former ages, and consequently unknown, they exalt almost into divinities, and honour as if they were their own immediate ancestors.

But even this devoted love of country is too narrow an emotion for the human soul. Man longs to live in the life of Humanity. Who does not know how even ordinary men are interested in fellow-creatures and events, far beyond the boundaries of their particular community; how their sympathies, aspirations and hopes extend to and embrace whatever Man is doing and suffering over the face of the whole earth? How do they become parties to conflicts of another hemisphere, confederates in heart with distant nations in their struggles and sacrifices, and glad witnesses of the progress of freedom and civilization throughout the world! How the daily newspapers are devoured by thousands and millions of readers, not for selfish ends of gain, or to discover channels through which they may pursue profitable enterprises, but simply from sympathy with men of every kindred and name, and anxiety to learn the fortunes and fate of Human Nature, throughout the vast movements of mankind! This same interest in the whole Human Race gives popularity to books of travel, whereby many, who have trodden no soil but their natal one, in spirit circumnavigate the globe, and establish friendly and fraternal acquaintance with the inhabitants alike of the tropics and the poles.

We have been speaking thus far of common men.
But when we rise to contemplate superior minds,
we find them peculiarly prompted to widen their
sympathies indefinitely, and to form close alliance
with their remotest brethren of the human race.
Literary and Scientific men, scattered abroad
through all nations, delight to multiply bonds of
scholarly union; learn eagerly one another's languages; liberally interchange thoughts and discoveries; form societies of exploration, observation
and historical and critical inquiry, to which the
most distant regions contribute members; and rejoice in the progress of knowledge as a common
cause. And through this citizenship of learned men
of all countries in one great Republic of Reason,
Science is now enlarging its conquests with a rapidity unexampled in former times. In like manner
Benevolent men, especially those who are consecrated to the same philanthropic objects, delight to
hear of the progress of Reforms in different nations;
rejoice that the grand Schemes of Benevolence, to
which they are devoted, enlist friends and helpers
far and wide; and exult in the success of its most
distant advocates, as truly as in their own.

Above all, is this conscious communion, in the
Life of Man Universal, profoundly felt in the sphere
of Religion. So susceptible is our social nature, that
the simple thought—that there are multitudes around
the globe who unite in a common religious faith,

hope and charity,—is all animating like an inspiration. The devout man worships with new zeal, when he feels that innumerable kindred souls are made one with his, in the love of the "One God and Father of all, who is above all, and through all, and in all,"—that this communion is not confined to our narrow world, but expands throughout all worlds into a glorious Temple, wherein God dwells; that in his hymns of praise he is echoing the anthems of Angelic choirs; that in his aspirations he is in unison with the emotions and joys of God's countless Spiritual Family throughout the Universe; and that he is even now a living member of an Immortal Organization, which is to grow ever more perfect, when the distinctions of nations, and even of humanity, will be dissolved in the love and joy of the holy and blessed Societies of Heaven.

II.—And now let us consider more nearly the extent of this Unity in the Church Universal,—how far it reaches, how many it embraces,—in order that we may gain a correspondent largeness and elevation of views and affections, of hopes and principles of action.

There is One Body and One Spirit. Christ has ONE CHURCH, not many Churches. All Christians are comprehended in One Community. However scattered, separated and divided,—in their fellowship with One Head, in their participation of One Faith and Spirit, they are attracted by a combining principle,—which, though counteracted **now,** can never be destroyed; and which will ultimately manifest itself in blending all believers, visibly and indissolubly, into One. From the very nature of the Christian Religion—as a Religion of Love—all who embrace it must be gathered into One Society. Christian Union cannot but be co-extensive with the Christian Religion, and diffused with it wherever it is spread. Such is the general doctrine of the text.

1. Now if all Christians constitute One Community only, then it is implied, not merely that Christians of the different denominations, which are scattered through the world, are nearly connected with one another here below, but that Christians on Earth and Christians in Heaven are livingly bound in fellowship. Being equally united to Christ, these two classes are necessarily comprehended in that One Body, which is quickened by the One Spirit of adoption, that animates the whole vast Family of the Children of God. Consequently they sustain most intimate relations with one another, instantly and everywhere.

It is common to speak of these two classes under the names of the Church Militant and the Church Triumphant. But these words merely denote the respective circumstances, amidst which different members of the same Community are for a season placed. The Church Militant and the Church

Triumphant are ONE Church; and the time is approaching in which these distinctions shall vanish away, and when all Christ's followers, crowned with the same triumph, shall be gathered into the same Visible Communion, around their common exalted Head. This doctrine is announced in a passage of singular magnificence and elevation, both of thought and language, in the Epistle to the Hebrews, where the writer says: "Ye are come unto Mount Sion, and unto the city of the Living God, the heavenly Jerusalem, and to an innumerable company of angels, to the general assembly and church of the first-born whose names are written in heaven, and to God the Judge of all, and to the spirits of just men made perfect." In other words, by unity of soul with Christ's Church, we are admitted into a real Communion of Saints, tender and confidential, which will gain strength and largeness as we and they advance towards celestial excellence.

2. If we consider, first, the position of Christians in Heaven,—who through life were devoutly interested in the growth of holiness and love among Christ's followers,—it is utterly incredible that they should cast off at death this form of benevolence, as if it were worth no more than the perishable body. For what is the Heaven, into which they have entered, but the Perfection of Charity, the unbroken harmony of all good affections? Although we may

well suppose that ties of a mere earthly nature will
fall from the purified spirit, yet attachments founded
in piety and goodness cannot but gather vigour as
souls mature in the Perfect Life. This doctrine of
the enduring sympathy, felt by Christians in Heaven
for Christians on Earth, should be placed beyond
doubt, if we believe that Christ's disciples ascend at
death into immediate personal intercourse with him.
You remember how Paul says, that "to be absent
from the body is to be present with the Lord."
Christians are not present with our Saviour merely
as we are with one another; for in the future state
the access of mind to mind must undoubtedly be
nearer than on earth. They have a communion
with his Spirit, such as the closest friendship does
not allow among imperfect men. Friendship is the
affection that predominates in the mind of Jesus.
Friendship is his very soul. We are assured that, in
his present glorified state, the same magnanimous
love, which upheld him in the agonies of crucifixion,
flows out continually towards his followers on earth,
and is manifested in perpetual efforts for their
progress and their final and complete redemption.
Christians in Heaven look with new clearness of
spiritual vision into the depth of this Love of Christ
"which passeth knowledge," until they too become
"filled with the fulness of God." And can we
imagine, that embosomed within this Divine Compassion, which is always descending from Heaven to

rth, and living in the midst of the warm and ttractive beams of this all-embracing Charity, they :an shake off concern for the Church below? Through closer adherence to the Head, can they become severed from the members, who are so dear and near to him as to be called "flesh of his flesh"?

I doubt not that Christians, who enter the Spiritual World, and attain to freedom from the alloy of selfishness, which tarnished their charity on earth, glow with a love of which we in our mortal state cannot distinctly conceive. We may gain a glimpse of it from the image given, when it is said, that "they shall shine as the Sun," that radiant minister of the Most High, who dwells in light. Who indeed can suppose that good men at death will grow cold to the Church, in the bosom of which they were themselves nurtured and bred for the heavenly community; that the martyrs who loved it more than life, and rose to heaven through flames, endured in its defence, should part with that zeal for its welfare to which they owe their crowns of glory? The fire of persecution could not consume, but only refined and exalted this divine zeal. I am persuaded that it is a great, however common an error, to conceive of the departed as so absorbed in their new mode of being as to forget their former one. To suppose them forgetful of the world, where they began to live, is to make that life worthless, and to blot out a volume of invaluable experience. To

think of them as regarding this world with indifference, when it was the scene of their Master's
life, and still bears the impress of his footsteps; when
it is associated so intimately with the manifestation
of his character, and is the object of his perpetual
care, is to make them dead to his glorious design of
good. Undoubtedly they think of our world with
very different feelings from those which it once ex-
cited. To them its splendours have paled amidst
the brightness of their new abode. The competi-
tions and strifes of men for a day's pre-eminence
seem to them childish, as well as sinful. This
world's grand interest to them is as the birthplace
of Immortal Minds, as the school where they are
trained for Heaven. But as such it is infinitely
precious, and they regard it with intense concern.

In these views we discover a peculiarity, and a
supremely honourable one, of the relationship
formed by Christianity among its disciples. It is
a perpetual and ever-growing relationship. The
toils and sufferings for a Nation,—which has its
date and is hastening to its appointed term; which
is soon to be joined, in its decline and fall, with
past and almost forgotten empires,—may fade from
the mind of the patriot. Death may break the bond
which joined him to it, and put an end not only to
his efforts for its welfare, but to his sympathies in its
fate. But not so can it be with the Christian.
Labourer and sufferer for the Church Universal as

he has been on earth, his energies are consecrated to an Immortal Cause; to the interests of a Community which will outlive sun and stars; and which, being of heavenly origin, tends towards and will be perfected in Heaven. Death cannot take him out of this Church, nor in the least degree loosen his connexions with it. On the contrary, he goes to join the triumphant, purified, blessed portion of this Community, among whom his affections for his militant brethren here, instead of being extinguished, will gain new fervour.

In regard to the methods in which Christians in the Spiritual World manifest their affections towards Christians on Earth,—in regard to the services and assistances they render,—I shall not attempt to speak. The doctrine, that they come to mortals as ministers of mercy; that in this mission they do the work of angels whom they resemble;—though reason in no way opposes it, and the heart welcomes it,—must be held, with a degree of uncertainty, as forming no part of revelation. But there is one office, by which the Risen and Glorified hold an active, beneficent, connexion with the Church on earth, of which we cannot doubt. With Christ's example before them, who is ever interceding for man,—and with the privilege of nearer access to God than they could enjoy in the body,—can we question that in their petitions they remember their tempted brethren, who are fighting that fight, of which by experience they know the toil and pain? Having prayed for the Church till their last breath, can we imagine that in their present exalted state, where intercession must be more effectual because springing from a purer heart, they should not mingle with their worship this high duty? Why should we think that prayer is confined to earth, or that its power of appeal can be weakened in heaven? Are Christians there denied the privilege, which is granted here, of invoking God's blessing on friends and brethren? For one, I doubt not that among the joyful praises of angels is heard a voice, less rapturous, but more tender, of affectionate intercession. Perhaps we shall hereafter find that no incense rises more acceptably before God's throne, than the prayers of Saints for their afflicted and endangered brethren in this state of probation. Thus have I given one illustration of the living ties between Christians in Heaven and Christians on Earth.

3. In the next place, how does the Christian on Earth contribute his part to this union? I answer, by recollection, and by hope; by looking back to the lives and characters of departed Saints while they were inhabitants of this world; and by anticipating joyfully their society in the world to come. The Christian, imbued with the spirit of his religion, maintains communion by grateful remembrance with

those who have gone before him, and especially with the more illustrious, whose holy services and sacrifices for the Church have crowned them with haloes of honour. He does not regard his Religion merely as a blessing of the present moment, but studies with profoundest interest its past history. He remembers that it has come down to him through a long procession of ages, and that it has been transmitted through the professions, sufferings, prayers and virtues of millions, who have lived and died for it before his birth. He delights to think of his Religion under the similitude, which Jesus gave, of a seed sown upon earth centuries ago, and to trace its growth,—nourished as it has been with the tears and sweat, the blood and anxious care, of the holiest persons in the records of the past. To the true Christian no history is so affecting, as that of the Church Universal. His soul unites with the pure and pious, who have clung to it in danger; who have fought beneath the banner of the Cross with spiritual weapons; who have conquered the powers of evil by self-sacrifice, suffering and death. The Apostle, bearing Christian truth through rude and barbarous nations to the ends of the earth, armed with the spirit of all-enduring and all-conquering love, rises before him,—high above conspicuous heroes and legislators,—as the most majestic and commanding form of human nature in the dim regions of anti-

quity. He feels his personal debt to the faith and
loyalty of these tried followers of Christ, and
blesses them for those labours of which he daily
reaps the fruits. Thus, by memory, we have connexion as truly with the Saints risen in glory, as
we have with those yet dwelling here. Though
dead, they still speak to us. And happy is it
for us when we open our minds to the influences
of the departed, and form intimacies with the great
and good who have preceded us into the world of
peace!

The Risen and Glorified thus speak to us from
distant regions and remote ages. But they speak
also from nearer times and more familiar scenes.
Indeed, there is no place in our own communities
and homes which is not consecrated by their blessed
images. How we delight to remember their ex-
cellencies; their superiority to this world's gifts;
their uncorrupted simplicity; the moderation with
which they enjoyed, the liberality with which they
imparted; the conscientiousness with which they
regarded themselves as the stewards of Divine mu-
nificence! The periods of their history to which
affection most gladly recurs are those in which they
manifested strength of principle that never faltered,
and fulness of love that never failed; when their
countenances glowed with lofty disinterestedness
and unconquerable trust in God. What an assured
conviction do we feel of the perpetuity and im-

mortality of such noble forms of goodness! What a certainty cheers us that these friends have ascended to a brighter world, when the serene spirit of that world had dawned upon their faces even in their earthly state! But when the Good leave us, it is not only to the more signal portions of their history that memory returns. We rejoice indeed to recall acts which deserved and won general admiration. But how delightful is it also to remember gentle, quiet, ceaseless virtues, which found their sphere in the seclusion of home, and spread a softened light through the privacy of domestic life; which perhaps no eye but our own witnessed, revealing to us a depth of piety and love such as no public conduct could display! How soothing are the recollections of the constancy of affection, that made sacrifices without knowing that they were such; which stifled its own griefs that it might not add to those of others; which bore the infirmities of friends as though it never saw them! How blessed is the remembrance of the unpretending devoutness, that made no outward profession, but mingled itself calmly and quietly with the whole tenor of thought and action, and shone forth steadily in resignation, persevering duty and unostentatious love!

The influence of the Good and Holy on the present world is thus not limited to their living in it. When are they so lovely, so winning, so powerful to guide and quicken, as after death has withdrawn them from us? Then we feel that the seal is set upon what was made Perfect in their souls. No more can they be sullied by contact with the earth. They take their place like stars in a region of purity and peace. They come to our thoughts clad in the light of celestial sanctity and sweetness. Shall we not follow them in thought to their high dwelling-place, and learn from them even diviner wisdom than they taught on earth?

Let us believe, too, that they carry with them all their recollections of the loved whom they have left behind. This earth, where they began the development of their moral being,—where they first heard the voice of conscience, felt their first love, fought their first conflicts, won their first triumphs, —must ever be endeared to them by most affecting associations. The friends who blessed them, and the friends whom they blessed, can never be banished from their minds. True, for a season they have parted from us; but they cannot forget us. The hearts which have felt for us so long, feel for us yet, more tranquilly indeed, but more profoundly. They love us still. We are objects of a holier interest than ever. And that interest is strengthened, in proportion as we grow in resemblance to the Ascended and Glorified, and fitter for their companionship.

But the Christian not only maintains a connexion

with his Brethren in Heaven by grateful recollections of their virtues. Still more closely is he
bound to them by hope. He does not remember them
as embalmed in history, to be known only through
the records of tradition. They still *live*, and are
members of the same Organic Body with himself.
Already he feels a brotherhood with them. He is
bound to them by more than distant admiration,
even by close and cordial friendship. Eagerly he
anticipates a future existence, because he shall meet
there the venerable dead, with whose Spirits, still
animating their biographies, histories and works,
he now communes. He rejoices to think of soon
hearing, seeing and holding familiar intercourse
with inspired Prophets and holy Poets, with Philanthropists and Sages, with Scholars and Artists, with
great-hearted Heroes of common life, whose characters and deeds have nourished in him pure purposes
and lofty aspirations ; and he is elevated towards their
sublime height by these soaring expectations. The
space that sunders him from them is daily growing
narrower ; and his present faint conceptions of them
will soon change into clear, full, intimate, personal
acquaintance. Steadfast in faith, he trusts that
they will receive and gladly incorporate him into
their society. Nor does he thus trust without good
grounds. Is there joy among the Angels over a
sinner who by repentance begins the Christian race,
and can we doubt that the arrival in heaven of a

20

spirit, which has finished its warfare and gained
the immortal crown, is blissful intelligence and an
event of transporting joy to its benevolent Communities ? This is indeed a glorious and glorifying
hope, that we shall be greeted with welcome by the
revered and illustrious, the humble and gentle, who
have gone before us into the world of light. But
let us not fear to yield to this high hope. For
the First among many Brethren will count his
work unfinished until his prayer shall be fulfilled,
that all who love and believe in him shall be one
with him, and with one another, as he and his
Father are one, and that where he is they shall
be also.

While speaking thus of the union between
Christians on Earth and Christians in Heaven by
hope, let me avow that my own impressions on this
subject were much strengthened by visiting Catholic
lands. I am aware that this admission may breed
suspicion of the soundness of my views. But we
ought not to doubt that among the corruptions of
the Catholic Church there are rich relics of primitive
truth. The zeal of the Reformation, too impetuous
and unsparing, rejected many principles and usages,
which deserve our respect and imitation. The
Catholic Church, it is well known, is distinguished
by the ardent veneration with which it cherishes
the memory and seeks the friendship of departed
Saints. And notwithstanding the superstitions

grafted upon this branch of their religion, they have done wisely in striving to multiply these germs from the Tree of Life, by perpetuating the examples of holy men and women, to whom Christianity was so largely indebted in its spring-time. I entered these countries with much of that indifference which has grown up among Protestants, through dread of Catholic abuses. But when, by the help of statuary and painting, my attention was awakened, and my mind brought to act on Christ's faithful followers in the early ages of the Church; when I beheld the celestial loveliness of his mother Mary; and especially when I contemplated the Martyr in his last hour, and saw, mysteriously mingled with the agonies of excruciating death, bright beams of immortal joy, indomitable trust, calm constancy, heroic courage, and meek forgiving charity—I felt the claim of these primitive disciples to our grateful love, as never before. I felt that, by death so endured, they had sent forth an influence to quicken all future times, and that they had become what they now are, everlastingly members of that Community of the Blessed to which I too aspire to belong. I rejoiced in being one with them by devotion to the same Head, and though now far separated in time, I longed one day to thank them for their loyalty to that Glorious Gospel, which has brightened all my hopes.

III.—My friends, I should not have insisted so

long upon this Communion between Christians in Heaven and Christians on Earth, did I not think this truth an eminently practical one. To many no lessons seem practical, except the minute inculcations of common duties. But, in fact, the most practical views in religion are those, which awaken the loftiest sentiments and touch the noblest springs of action. And the subject, now discussed, is peculiarly fitted to give life and energy to our convictions of the Spiritual World, and to lift our minds above the sordid mood, into which they are so prone to sink. The attraction of Heaven lies in the Beings who reside there. And whilst the thought of the Presence of God is enough to inflame intense desire, yet we are greatly aided by conceiving of Our Father's House as the mansion of all the excellent, whose lives have sanctified the earth. In proportion, as in thought, we commune with this "Assembly and Church of the Firstborn," we learn to revere our own spiritual capacities, which can alone fit us for such high society.

Unhappily speculations of this nature seem to many not only wanting in practical utility, but as unreal fictions of the fancy. Whatever goes beyond our present experience passes with such for visionary and romantic. The Spiritual World is to them a void. And the idea of Higher Orders of Beings, though so plainly revealed in Scripture, and attested by all Traditions, gains from them merely a half sceptical assent. But if Revelation be worthy of any credit, the intercourse between Heaven and Earth is most close and constant. Jesus Christ, Risen and Glorified,—who once lived here below,— now *lives* on high, not as an unconcerned Spectator, but as a mighty Agent for the good of the whole human race. Angels, commissioned by his boundless love, he sends forth to minister to all heirs of salvation. Near him are Christians, who, departed from this world in faith, now sympathize and cowork with him in promoting the growth of his ever-expanding Community. And to the mind that can shake off the clogs of earth, and freely exercise its spiritual powers, these views will appear to be as sober and rational, as they are joyful and exalting.

How unparalleled in dignity is the Church Universal, as we have now contemplated it! In extent it surpasses all other communities, gathering in its wide embrace Spirits made Perfect around the throne of God, Holy Men in heaven, and the Children of the Father throughout all nations. And as to duration, not only has it withstood the shocks of ages,—outlasting Empires and States amidst which it has been planted, and still flourishing with perennial growth while they decay;—but it is appointed to survive the present order of the Natural World, and to be transformed from glory to glory in regions of the Universe beyond all

adverse change. How cheering is this confidence
that we are even now citizens of a Kingdom that
can never be moved, members of a Community
that is organized by a principle of Imperishable
Life!

When, by an act of faith and hope, we transport
ourselves into the world, where Human Nature is
redeemed from every sin and woe, and there behold
the good, the just, the wise, the lovely, trained in
all regions and ages,—a multitude which no man
can number,—exalted to new life, new powers, new
friendships, new prospects of the immense creation, and new ministries of love in co-operation with
higher beings and with God,—then does the awful
grandeur of Immortality open before us; then do we
feel, with devout gratitude, that this birth-place and
school for Spirits is worthy of its Divine Author,
and of its sublime consummation.

"Compassed about by this great cloud of Witnesses," let us with firm and cheerful trust endure
all trials, discharge all duties, accept all sacrifices,
fulfil the law of universal and impartial love, and
adopt as our own that cause of truth, righteousness,
humanity, liberty and holiness,—which, being the
cause of the All-Good, cannot but triumph over all
powers of evil. Let us rise into blest assurance that
everywhere and for ever we are enfolded, penetrated,
guarded, guided, kept by the power of the Father
and Friend, who can never forsake us; and that all

Spirits who have begun to seek, know, love and serve the All-Perfect One on earth, shall be re-united in a Celestial Home, and be welcomed together into the Freedom of the Universe, and the Perpetual Light of His Presence!

THE END.

CPSIA information can be obtained
at www.ICGtesting.com
Printed in the USA
BVOW06s0740300917

496375BV00012B/512/P

9 781330 516027